IA®

How to access your on-line resources

Kaplan Financial students will have a MyKaplan account and these extra resources will be available to you online. You do not need to register again, as this process was completed when you enrolled. If you are having problems accessing online materials, please ask your course administrator.

If you are not studying with Kaplan and did not purchase your book via a Kaplan website, to unlock your extra online resources please go to www.en-gage.co.uk (even if you have set up an account and registered books previously). You will then need to enter the ISBN number (on the title page and back cover) and the unique pass key number contained in the scratch panel below to gain access.

You will also be required to enter additional information during this process to set up or confirm your account details.

If you purchased via the Kaplan Publishing website you will automatically receive an e-mail invitation to register your details and gain access to your content. If you do not receive the e-mail or book content, please contact Kaplan Publishing.

Your code and information

This code can only be used once for the registration of one book online. This registration and your online content will expire when the final sittings for the examinations covered by this book have taken place. Please allow one hour from the time you submit your book details for us to process your request.

Please scratch the film to access your unique code.

Please be aware that this code is case-sensitive and you will need to include the dashes within the passcode, but not when entering the ISBN.

KAPLAN

PUBLISHING

CIMA

Case Study

Operational Level

Study Text

Published by: Kaplan Publishing UK

Unit 2 The Business Centre, Molly Millars Lane, Wokingham, Berkshire RG41 2QZ

Acknowledgements

We are grateful to the CIMA for permission to reproduce past examination questions and the official CIMA answers.

Notice

British Library Cataloguing in Publication Data

A catalogue record for this book is available from the British Library.

ISBN: 978-1-78740-202-7

Printed and bound in Great Britain

Contents

		Page
Chapter 1	Introduction to case study exams	1
Chapter 2	Core activities and assessment outcomes	11
Chapter 3	2019 Prototype exam – pre-seen information	59
Chapter 4	2019 Prototype exam – analysing the pre-seen	81
Chapter 5	Exam day techniques	103
Chapter 6	2019 Prototype exam – walkthrough of variant 1	117
Chapter 7	Feedback on the real exam and tips on answering the more technical aspects of P1 and F1	143

Introduction

Acknowledgements

Every effort has been made to contact the holders of copyright material, but if any here have been inadvertently overlooked the publishers will be pleased to make the necessary arrangements at the first opportunity.

How to use the Materials

 Test your understanding – Following key points and definitions are exercises which give the opportunity to assess the understanding of these core areas. Within the work book the answers to these sections are left blank, explanations to the questions can be found within the online version which can be hidden or shown on screen to enable repetition of activities.

 Illustration – to help develop an understanding of topics and the test your understanding exercises the illustrative examples can be used.

Quality and accuracy are of the utmost importance to us so if you spot an error in any of our products, please send an email to mykaplanreporting@kaplan.com with full details.

Our Quality Coordinator will work with our technical team to verify the error and take action to ensure it is corrected in future editions.

Exam Introduction

To complete the CIMA qualification and be able to use the designatory letters of ACMA and CGMA, candidates for this prestigious award need to achieve three things:

- attain the entry requirements for the professional level qualification
- study for and complete the relevant professional level assessments and examinations
- complete three years of relevant practical experience

This text concentrates on the second of these requirements, and in particular to study for and complete the Operational level case study exam.

Overview of exam

The case study exam will be available four times a year. The purpose of this exam is to consolidate learning at each level by reflecting real life work situations. The exam is human marked.

This approach allows a wide range of knowledge and skills to be tested including research and analysis, presentation of information and communication skills whilst still ensuring competence in key skills.

CIMA believe that this format will provide the commitment to delivering the competencies which employers desire thereby improving 'employability'.

For example, the Operational level case study exam will be set within a simulated business context, placing the candidate in the job role matched to the competency level. In the case of the Operational level, the job role is that of an entry level finance professional (usually a management accountant) with responsibility for some of the consequences of implementing strategy. The focus will be on the short-term.

Typical aspects of such a role could include the following:

- An understanding of costs and cost accounting, in order to start preparing budgets, and to advise about short-term changes in products, volume and prices.
- Putting budgets together for the business will require communicating aspects of the budget to non-finance staff; both in the preparation and the delivery.
- Preparation of financial reports to show how the business is performing. This will require knowledge of the regulatory environment, financial reporting, and business taxation.
- Analysing and advising on working capital, cash and short-term finance.

The exam is intended to replicate "a day in the life" of a finance professional operating at the operational level and provide a simulated environment for candidates to demonstrate the required level of proficiency in each of the competency areas. Consequently, the exam will be set and marked according to the weightings for each core activity at the level.

The case study exam is 3 hours in duration and is made up of a series of timed tests or tasks. This makes the case study exam different from most exams you will have sat to date – once you have submitted a particular task (or the time limit is reached, whichever is sooner) you will be moved on and will not be able to return to that task. This should reduce the problem of not completing the paper but does mean you will need to be very disciplined when attempting each task.

Candidates will be provided with access to pre-seen information approximately seven weeks before the real exam.

Assessment aims and strategy

The Case Study Examination tests the knowledge, skills and techniques from the three pillars within one simulated scenario and is taken at the end of each level of the CIMA Professional Qualification. Candidates are given a fictional Case Study before the examination and are expected to give solutions to the situations and challenges presented within the examination – based on the knowledge and skills acquired from the three subjects. The Case Study mimics their role in a real-work scenario, at each level of the qualification.

The case study is three hours long. The case study will include both pre-seen and unseen material, the latter being made available during the examination. They will incorporate short written answers, emails, letters and any form of appropriate communication required within the tasks set.

The focus is on application, analysis and evaluation which are levels 3, 4 and 5 of the CIMA hierarchy of verbs (see below).

Simulated business issues in the case studies provide candidates with the opportunity to demonstrate their familiarity with the context and interrelationships of the level's technical content. This reflects the cross functional abilities required in the workplace. Skills will include research, analysis, and presentation of both financial and nonfinancial information and communication skills.

Feedback will be provided to candidates with their results. Exam sittings for the case studies will occur every three months. Candidates must have completed or be exempt from the three objective tests at a particular level before attempting the relevant case study.

Core activities and assessment outcomes

Within each Operational Case Study Examination, six "core activities" will be assessed. These core activities represent the tasks that are most frequent, critical and important to the entry level finance professional role.

The six core activities are:

A   Prepare costing information for different purposes to meet the needs of management.

B   Prepare budget information and assess its use for planning and control purposes.

C   Analyse performance using financial and non- financial information.

D   Apply relevant financial reporting standards and corporate governance, ethical and tax principles.

E   Prepare information to support short-term decision-making.

F   Prepare information to manage working capital.

The core activities require and draw together the knowledge, skills and techniques acquired while studying for Objective Tests and combining them with the mindset of a CIMA finance professional.

Each core activity is translated into a number of "assessment outcomes". These are a clear assertion of what a CIMA qualified finance professional should be able to do when the Examination has been completed and what the assessment will be designed to measure. Case Study assessment outcomes will be synoptic

These are discussed in more detail in chapters 1 and 2.

Assessing skills – the CIMA verb hierarchy

CIMA has adopted a skill framework for the assessments based on the revised Bloom's Taxonomy of Education Objectives. Bloom's Taxonomy classifies a continuum of skills that learners are expected to know and demonstrate.

The case study exam will focus on Levels 3, 4 and 5.

Skill level	Verbs used	Definition
Level 5 Evaluation How you are expected to use your learning to evaluate, make decisions or recommendations	Advise	Counsel, inform or notify
	Assess	Evaluate or estimate the nature, ability or quality of
	Evaluate	Appraise or assess the value of
	Recommend	Propose a course of action
	Review	Assess and evaluate in order, to change if necessary
Level 4 Analysis How you are expected to analyse the detail of what you have learned	Align	Arrange in an orderly way
	Analyse	Examine in detail the structure of
	Communicate	Share or exchange information
	Compare and contrast	Show the similarities and/or differences between
	Develop	Grow and expand a concept
	Discuss	Examine in detail by argument
	Examine	Inspect thoroughly
	Interpret	Translate into intelligible or familiar terms
	Monitor	Observe and check the progress of
	Prioritise	Place in order of priority or sequence for action
	Produce	Create or bring into existence
Level 3 Application How you are expected to apply your knowledge	Apply	Put to practical use
	Calculate	Ascertain or reckon mathematically
	Conduct	Organise and carry out
	Demonstrate	Prove with certainty or exhibit by practical means
	Prepare	Make or get ready for use
	Reconcile	Make or prove consistent/compatible
Level 2 Comprehension What you are expected to understand	Describe	Communicate the key features of
	Distinguish	Highlight the differences between
	Explain	Make clear or intelligible/state the meaning or purpose of
	Identify	Recognise, establish or select after consideration
	Illustrate	Use an example to describe or explain something
Level 1 Knowledge What you are expected to know	List	Make a list of
	State	Express, fully or clearly, the details/facts of
	Define	Give the exact meaning of
	Outline	Give a summary of

How to use the material

These Official CIMA learning materials brought to you by CIMA and Kaplan Publishing have been carefully designed to make your learning experience as easy as possible and give you the best chances of success in your Case Study Examinations.

This Study Text has been designed with the needs of home study and distance learning candidates in mind. However, the Study Text is also ideal for fully taught courses.

The aim of this textbook is to walk you through the stages to prepare for, and to answer, the requirements of the Case Study Examination.

Practical hints and realistic tips are given throughout the book making it easy for you to apply what you've learned in this text to your actual Case Study Exam.

Where sample solutions are provided, they must be viewed as just one interpretation of the case. One key aspect, which you must appreciate early in your studies, is that there is no single 'correct' solution.

Your own answer might reach different conclusions, and give greater emphasis to some issues and less emphasis to others, but score equally as well if it demonstrates the required skills.

If you work conscientiously through the official CIMA Study Text according to the guidelines above, as well as analysing the pre-seen information in full, you will be giving yourself an excellent chance of success in your examination. Good luck with your studies!

Planning

To begin with, formal planning is essential to get the best return from the time you spend studying. Estimate how much time in total you are going to need for each subject you are studying for the Case Study Examination. You may find it helpful to read "Pass First Time!" second edition by David R. Harris ISBN 978-1-85617-798-6.

This book will provide you with proven study techniques. Chapter by chapter it covers the building blocks of successful learning and examination techniques and shows you how to earn all the marks you deserve, and explains how to avoid the most common pitfalls.

With your study material before you, decide which chapters you are going to study in each week, which weeks you will devote to practising past exams, and which weeks you will spend becoming familiar with your case study pre-seen material.

Prepare a written schedule summarising the above and stick to it! Students are advised to refer to articles published regularly in CIMA's magazine (Financial Management), the student e-newsletter (Velocity) and on the CIMA website, to ensure they are up to date with relevant issues and topics.

Tips for effective studying

1   Aim to find a quiet and undisturbed location for your study, and plan as far as possible to use the same period of time each day. Getting into a routine helps to avoid wasting time. Make sure that you have all the materials you need before you begin so as to minimise interruptions.

2   Store all your materials in one place, so that you do not waste time searching for items every time you want to begin studying. If you have to pack everything away after each study period, keep your study materials in a box, or even a suitcase, which will not be disturbed until the next time.

3   Limit distractions. To make the most effective use of your study periods you should be able to apply total concentration, so turn off all entertainment equipment, set your phones to message mode, and put up your 'do not disturb' sign.

4   Your timetable will tell you which topic to study. However, before diving in and becoming engrossed in the finer points, make sure you have an overall picture of all the areas that need to be covered by the end of that session. After an hour, allow yourself a short break and move away from your Study Text. With experience, you will learn to assess the pace you need to work at. Each study session should focus on component learning outcomes – the basis for all questions.

5   Work carefully through a chapter, making notes as you go. When you have covered a suitable amount of material, vary the pattern by attempting a practice question. When you have finished your attempt, make notes of any mistakes you made, or any areas that you failed to cover or covered more briefly. Be aware that all component learning outcomes will be tested in each examination.

6   Make notes as you study, and discover the techniques that work best for you. Your notes may be in the form of lists, bullet points, diagrams, summaries, 'mind maps', or the written word, but remember that you will need to refer back to them at a later date, so they must be intelligible. If you are on a taught course, make sure you highlight any issues you would like to follow up with your lecturer.

7   Organise your notes. Make sure that all your notes, calculations etc. can be effectively filed and easily retrieved later.

Relevant practical experience

In order to become a Chartered Global Management Accountant (ACMA, CGMA), you need a minimum of three years' verified relevant work-based practical experience.

Read the 'Applying for Membership' brochure for full details of the practical experience requirements (PER).

Information concerning formulae and tables will be provided via the CIMA website, www.cimaglobal.com, and your EN-gage login.

Introduction to case study exams

Chapter learning objectives

- To gain an overview of the case study exam, its purpose, structure and the process involved.

1 The structure of the CIMA Operational Level

Each level of CIMA's professional qualification consists of three objective test 'pillar' exams, followed by the Case Study Examination.

You can only attempt the Case Study Examination after all objective tests for the level have been completed or if exemptions have been given.

For the 2019 syllabus the three Operational level pillar exams are as follows:

- E1 – Managing Finance in a Digital World
- P1 – Management Accounting
- F1 – Financial Reporting

The objective tests for each of these individual subjects ensure the acquisition of the breadth of knowledge, skills and techniques that provide the foundation for approaching the Case Study Examination.

2 Why a Case Study Examination?

The CIMA Case Study Examinations are 'capstone' examinations designed to demonstrate mastery of previously acquired knowledge, skills and techniques and the drawing together of these to provide solutions to unstructured, synoptic problems.

Each synoptic assessment combines the content covered in all three pillar subjects at the level into a single assessment. Its aim is the "undoing" of the pillar and subject divisions of the syllabus and the application of knowledge, skills and techniques to the type of problems that you might encounter in the workplace in a role matched to the appropriate level of the qualification.

The examination uses a simulated Case Study to provide a rich, immersive scenario to prepare and to provide a context for the tasks in the examination. The scenarios are developed around today's modern business environment and the challenges that you will face – allowing you to demonstrate the 'core activities' that have been identified by employers as critical.

Examination tasks will be practical and applied, not theoretical or academic. To be successful, you will have to perform these core activities in the same way and to the same standards that would be valid and valued in the workplace.

The Case Study Examination is thus an attempt to simulate workplace problem solving, and allows examiners to move one step closer to the assessment of competence than is possible with objective test questions. It is a test of both professional competence and, by implication, employability.

In addition, the purpose of the Case Study Examination is to assess your proficiency in those specific skills that are less likely to be automated.

The purpose of this text is to suggest how you might prepare for the examination by developing and practising your skills. Since the examination tests a range of different skills, preparing for this examination needs to be different from studying for a 'traditional' examination.

3   Your role

Each case study exam will be set within a simulated business context, placing the candidate in the job role matched to the competency level.

In the case of the operational level your role is an entry level finance professional or a finance officer, typically a management accountant, reporting to first line managers and/or peers within the organisation.

This role can be broken down as follows:

- The role simulated is that of a finance officer working within a collaborative team in the finance department that is responsible for planning and coordinating business operations through the preparation of budgets and other reports. The role focuses on the short term; assisting with the preparation of useful and relevant financial reports, drawing upon data collected by the company's information system. The finance officer may be asked to evaluate short-term opportunities and threats, such as selecting between alternative courses of action and may also provide information to support decisions on working capital, cash and short-term finance.

- The finance officer offers insights that influence the decisions taken by her colleagues and superiors. The finance officer must act in a professional manner, ensuring that her reports are sufficiently complete and accurate to facilitate decisions.

- The finance officer makes full use of the technologies that are available for the collection, cleansing and analysis of data. The preparation of reports also relies heavily on understanding of how the business is structured. The finance officer is required to interact with colleagues from finance and all other functional areas of the business.

- The finance officer also assists in the preparation of financial reports to enable external stakeholders to understand how the business is performing. That requires an understanding of the regulations relating to financial reporting and business taxation.

- The fact that the finance officer's work affects the behaviour of internal and external stakeholders can raise ethical implications. The finance officer must be aware of personal responsibilities working within the role.

In summary, the Operational level focuses on the short term and the implementation of decisions. Thus you will work with others in the organisation and use appropriate data and technology to translate medium- term decisions into short-term actionable plans.

The competency level is described as "entry-level", requiring you to demonstrate the ability to analyse and advise on various aspects and consequences of the implementation of strategy.

4   The exam 'blueprints'

For the first time, CIMA has released blueprints for its Professional Qualification Examination. The intent is that blueprints will demystify the examination – giving greater clarity on examinable topics; assessment approach, design and weightings; and learner expectations.

The Case Study Examination blueprint contains the following:

- **Core activities** – Business-related tasks that are common to the role being simulated and valued by employers which, if performed satisfactorily, enables the demonstration of the assessment outcomes.

- **Assessment outcomes** – A clear assertion of what a CIMA qualified finance professional can do when the Examination has been completed and what the assessment will be designed to measure. Case Study assessment outcomes will be synoptic.

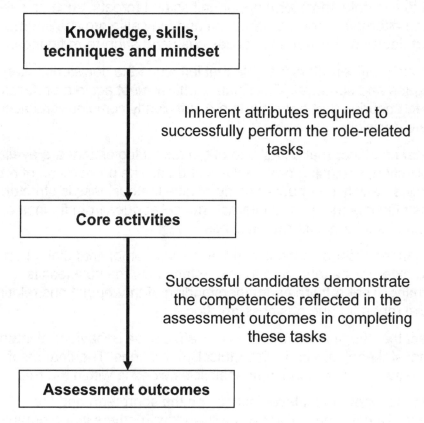

All core activities will be assessed in each form of the examination in line with the weightings. A sample of related assessment outcomes will be tested.

Blueprints are discussed in more detail in chapter 2.

5 The exam process

5.1 Overview

The examination is three hours long. A 15-minute tutorial is available before the start of the examination to allow candidates to familiarise themselves with the test driver.

The examination has four sections (tasks), which are each 45 minutes long. All sections are equally weighted. Candidates may finish a section early and move on to the next but cannot return to previous sections in the time remaining.

There may be more than one sub-task within each section and an indication of how long to spend on each sub-task will be given to allow candidates to manage their time.

For example, the first exam variant of the sample prototype paper shows the following instructions:

Section (task)	Time for section (minutes)	Number of answer screens	Number of sub-tasks	% time to spend on each sub-task
1	45	1	2	(a) 48% (b) 52%
2	45	1	2	(a) 52% (b) 48%
3	45	1	2	(a) 36% (b) 64%
4	45	1	2	(a) 60% (b) 40%

More than one core activity will normally (but not always) be assessed in each section/task and the order of core activities and assessment outcomes in the blueprint does not reflect how these might be structured in the examination.

For each sitting there are a number of variants, so different students will not necessarily face the same exam tasks. You are not permitted to discuss any aspects of the variant you sat until after the exam window has finished. The marking and moderation processes ensure that no advantage is gained from sitting one particular variant rather than another.

5.2 The pre-seen

The exam is based on:

- pre-seen material issued in advance of the exam day, supplemented by

- additional, previously unseen material given to you in the exam room.

From the May 2020 sitting onwards, one pre-seen will be used over two exam windows, giving candidates the opportunity to resit using the same pre-seen. The pre-seen will be shared as follows:

- May / August

- November / February

CIMA releases the pre-seen material approximately seven weeks before the first examination. This is posted on the student area of the CIMA website (www.cimaglobal.com) and it is your responsibility to download it and to print off a copy.

The pre-seen material is an introductory scenario to set the scene for the case study, together with accounting and financial information. The pre-seen material is an extended scenario consisting of approximately ten exhibits giving information about a business organisation.

You will be taking on the role of a management accountant who works for the organisation, and your responses to the tasks will usually be addressed to your superior.

5.3 The unseen

In the examination you will be provided with the following.

- An on-screen version of the pre-seen material

- Additional new unseen material, which contains both triggers (new information) and tasks (what you need to do)

- Space to complete your answers

- An on-screen calculator (although candidates are permitted to take their own calculators as long as it's a CIMA approved model.)

- Reference materials (Present value tables, Cumulative present value tables and Normal distribution tables)

- A notepad and pen for planning and workings along with an on-screen scratch pad.

The unseen material will be a continuation of the pre-seen and will usually bring the scenario up to date. In many cases there is a 'twist' in the unseen i.e. a development that students might not have anticipated from the pre-seen. The unseen may focus on a number of issues that appeared in the pre-seen or it may just focus on one or two; either way it will provide the basis for the content of your answers.

A common mistake made by weaker students is that they place too much emphasis on their analysis of the pre-seen material and do not develop the information in the unseen material adequately. The key points to be referred to in your answer should be driven by the new information in the unseen material.

5.4 Triggers and tasks

Each section in the unseen material will begin with a **trigger.**

This will be information provided as an introduction to the work that you are required to complete.

The information may be in the form of a briefing by your superior, a newspaper article, some financial information or extracts from internal reports. You will be expected to integrate this new information with the analysis you have performed on the pre-seen material to produce a coherent and well informed response.

Within each section of the examination, there will then be a **task** or tasks that you will be asked to perform, usually by your superior. These tasks will require different types of response, although usually reports, briefing notes and emails.

Word processing capabilities will be provided within the test driver to allow the formatting and presentation of responses in a professional manner. From 2019, this includes the ability to use tables to put together a response. For full details of the word processing functionality and to try this in advance of the examination, a tutorial is available on cimaglobal.com.

There is a time limit attached to each task and you will have a clock showing the time remaining in the corner of your screen. Once you have submitted a task (or the time limit is reached, whichever is sooner) you will not be able to return to that task. This should reduce the problem of not completing the paper but does mean you will need to be disciplined when attempting each task.

If you feel that you do not need all of the time on an earlier task, then moving forwards prematurely will not allow you extra time on later tasks – the extra time will be lost. Given this, it is always advisable to use the full time allocated to each task to recheck that you have answered the question requirement in full and that you have related your response to the specific context of the case.

A walkthrough of the prototype sample exam will be carried out in chapters 3 to 5.

5.5 Calculations

Examination tasks will not be set that require specific calculations.

However, candidates should, wherever possible, show how they have used and interpreted data from the pre-seen and the new information presented during the examination and/or undertook analysis or calculations to support their responses.

6   Marking

6.1 Overview

The Case Study Examinations are human marked. The Case Study results will contain the following information:

- Grade: Pass or fail
- Scaled score: 0 to 150 with 80 and above being a pass

There is no requirement to obtain a pass or meet a minimum threshold for each core activity.

Feedback on performance against each core activity will be provided so that learners know their areas of weakness for further study.

Grade descriptors for both the overall passing standard as well as each core activity will also be released.

6.2 The 'marginally competent' student

During 2016 CIMA disclosed further information on how the pass mark is set and the importance of identifying the 'marginally competent' student.

The process

A detailed process was revealed that involves the following:

(1)   A panel of experts debates the tasks within a variant to decide what should be expected from a student deemed competent for this task. This debate does not focus on a perfect answer but, instead, asks what would be expected of a CIMA student (or member) in practice – what is the minimum expected if we were considering employing them, for example.

(2)   A sample of student scripts is then discussed and the scripts ranked. This is repeated and refined until the "marginally competent student" is identified. This student deserves to pass (but only just!) as they would be employable and have the skills expected of a CIMA student or member in the real world.

(3)   The marks earned by this script are then used to set the pass mark and standardise the overall marking system. This ensures that students are not disadvantaged if they sit a "harder" variant.

The lessons to be learned

When answering a task in the exam, you could imagine that this was part of a job interview and ask yourself what would be required to get the job.

Your employer would be less impressed by you showing off knowledge but much more impressed that you can answer a question asked, apply your comments to the company's specific circumstances and make practical, relevant suggestions. Make sure your answers do this!

7 Summary

You should now have a basic understanding of how the case study works. All of the ideas presented in this chapter will be developed further in the remainder of this textbook.

Next steps:

(1) It is a good idea to register with Pearson Vue to see the online version of the "Question tutorial" exam as this will allow you become more familiar with the look and feel of the exam. All the relevant material from the "Question tutorial" exam has been reproduced in this textbook but it is important to recognise that the CIMA case study examinations are dynamic and shouldn't be viewed as equivalent to a static paper exam.

(2) Think about the date on which you will sit the exam and work backwards to create a sensible and achievable study timetable.

(3) You need to ensure that your technical knowledge is up to date / full especially if the OTQ exams were sat a while ago.

It might be worth locating and gathering together any materials you already have from the supporting technical subjects (E1, P1 and F1). We will show you in later chapters how you may need to use these materials.

Core activities and assessment outcomes

Chapter learning objectives

- To understand the core activities and assessment outcomes required for the case study exam.

1   Core Activities

In some respects one could argue that everything covered in E1, F1 and P1 was still relevant for the Case Study Examination. However, to make such a daunting proposition more accessible and clear, the blueprint defines the following core activities:

	Core Activity	Weighting
A	Prepare costing information for different purposes to meet the needs of management.	12–18%
B	Prepare budget information and assess its use for planning and control purposes.	17–25%
C	Analyse performance using financial and non-financial information.	17–25%
D	Apply relevant financial reporting standards and corporate governance, ethical and tax principles.	12–18%
E	Prepare information to support short-term decision-making.	17–25%
F	Prepare information to manage working capital.	7–13%

As stated in chapter 1, **all** core activities will be assessed in each form of the examination in line with the weightings.

These core activities are linked to associated assessment outcomes expressed in terms of 'I Can' statements that speak directly to the skills and competencies that drive the employability of successful learners.

At first sight it may seem that core activities A, B, C and E are driven mainly by P1 knowledge and activities D and F by F1. Given this, you may wonder how E1 fits into this framework and the answer is that, rather than having a dedicated core activity for E1 content, key aspects of E1 are embedded within the other activities. This is seen more clearly when we look at the underlying assessment outcomes below.

2   Assessment outcomes

Assessment outcomes translate core activities into a range of "I can" statements that, in case study, effectively give you the basis of the wordings for exam tasks.

Given this, it is vital that you look at the assessment outcomes and make sure you feel confident that you could answer a task worded in this way. The full list is as follows:

	Core Activities	Assessment outcomes
A	Prepare costing information for different purposes to meet the needs of management.	I can use appropriate technologies to gather data for costing purposes, from digital and other sources. I can apply different costing methods to produce costing information suitable for managers' needs. I can explain costing information to operational and senior management using appropriate formats and media. I can compare different costing methods and systems to determine the most suitable for use by the organisation for different purposes. I can identify the cost information required for digital cost objects.
B	Prepare budget information and assess its use for planning and control purposes.	I can use appropriate technologies to gather data from digital and other sources to co-ordinate budget preparation. I can explain and use different forecasting methods to assist in budget preparation. I can use different approaches to produce information for use by managers when preparing budgets. I can explain budget information to managers using appropriate formats and media. I can apply various techniques to determine the effect on budgets of changes to variables. I can explain to functional managers how budgets are used for planning and control purposes. I can discuss the behavioural implications of budgetary planning and control. I can compare alternative approaches to budgeting to determine their suitability for the organisation and for different purposes.

C	Analyse performance using financial and non-financial information.	I can identify information that can enable managers to review performance.
		I can interpret variances to review functional and organisational performance.
		I can identify appropriate KPIs for different functions of the organisation.
		I can explain company performance using KPIs.
		I can prepare performance reports for use by different functions and for different purposes in appropriate formats and media.
D	Apply relevant financial reporting standards and corporate governance, ethical and tax principles.	I can apply relevant IFRS in a given context, to facilitate the preparation of financial statements.
		I can apply the principles of corporate governance and ethics.
		I can identify the impact of tax regulation on transactions, decisions and profits.
E	Prepare information to support short-term decision-making.	I can identify relevant costs and benefits.
		I can apply appropriate techniques that support short-term decision-making.
		I can prepare information to support operational decisions.
		I can explain factors that could influence short-term decisions.
		I can apply appropriate techniques to deal with situations where there is risk and uncertainty.
F	Prepare information to manage working capital.	I can identify appropriate sources of short-term finance and methods of short-term investments.
		I can explain how to manage and control working capital.
		I can explain working capital ratios in comparison to prior periods or to other organisations.
		I can identify the impact of changing working capital policies.

In the next section we will look at how these have been examined in the real exam. Given the syllabus changes in 2019, some tasks in past exams are no longer relevant, so we have focussed on ones that are still indicative of what you might face in your exam.

3 Examples of tasks from the August 2018 exam.

3.1 Summary of pre-seen scenario

To fully appreciate examples from recent real exams it is necessary to have a basic understanding of the two cases concerned.

The pre-seen information for August 2018 concerns a company called Thomas Fine Teas that produces tea bags in the country of Deeland.

Business model

At present, Thomas Fine Teas imports premium quality tea leaves from around the world and creates its own distinctive blends.

Expert tasters and blenders are employed to ensure that premium tasting leaves are sourced and then blended in such a way as to ensure that each batch of a particular blend always tastes the same.

The company has built up a strong reputation in Deeland and so can charge higher than average prices.

Channel strategy

Thomas Fine Teas currently sells its products to all four large supermarket chains in Deeland, two wholesalers and to four large corporate clients.

The main opportunity for growth in terms of channel strategy is within the corporate market (unless Thomas Fine Teas decides to start selling to smaller independent retailers or into other countries).

Product portfolio performance

The tea market is split in the pre-seen into three main segments – black teas, green teas and infusions.

- Black teas make up 58% of Thomas Fine Teas' budgeted sales and the company has an 11.3% (by volume) share of the Deeland market. Unfortunately this market is expected to be static or even decline going forwards.

- The market for green teas is expected to grow by around 5-6% a year but it is disappointing that, while being a pioneer of green teas in Deeland, Thomas Fine Teas has seen its market share fall from 25% to 16.5% in five years. Despite this, green teas still make up 22% of budgeting revenue.

- Similarly, the market for infusions, which make up 20% of budgeted sales, is also expected to grow by 5-6% a year. Again, Thomas Fine Teas was once at the forefront of encouraging consumers to drink infusions but has seen its market share fall from 20% to 5% in five years.

There are two main reasons for this downward trend in market share of green teas and infusions:

- The main problem has been a lack of product development and, in many respects the Board could be accused of complacency. It has been 10 years since a new green tea blend was launched and 15 years since a new range of infusions was released into the market. This is completely at odds with the increasing demand in green teas and infusions for new flavour combinations.

- The other reason for declining market share of green teas and infusions has been Thomas Fine Teas' commitment to only using traditional forms of advertising whereas the growth segments are with younger customers and those people trying to live a healthier lifestyle. Both are likely to respond better to digital marketing campaigns, viral advertising and the use of social media.

Financial performance

Revenue grew by 5.4% from 2017 to 2016, resulting in an increase of 14% in operating profit. This also increased operating margins from 14.5% to 15.8%.

The overall level of investment in non-current assets fell, again suggesting a lack of ambition by the Board.

In terms of working capital and liquidity, an additional D$3.5 million was tied up in working capital at the end of the year. Inventory days and receivables stayed fairly constant but the receivables days figure (>100 days) seems excessive given Thomas Fine Teas specifies a credit period of 30 days.

Budgeting

Budgets are prepared on an annual basis and incorporate a standard absorption costing system where overheads are absorbed using direct labour hours. Thomas Fine Teas adopts a participative approach, which should give better ownership of budgets but may result in budgetary 'slack' and 'padding'.

Budgeted sales for 2019 give an increase in revenue of 3.5% over 2018 but we are not told how this was determined / justified.

Future challenges

Thomas Fine Teas faces a number of key challenges.

Firstly it needs to invest in new product development for green teas and infusions. The company is currently over-reliant on black teas, a market segment with little or no growth prospects

Secondly, it needs to reconsider its marketing approach and how best to target younger people and those seeking a healthier lifestyle.

Thirdly it needs to consider how best to manage large powerful customers, such as supermarket chains. At the moment Thomas Fine Teas seems to have the edge when it comes to pricing but the fact that receivables days is over 100 days would indicate that the company is not having everything its own way.

3.2 Example tasks

In the real exam each task typically covers two core activities. For simplicity we have separated these out to highlight individual assessment outcomes. Answers are given at the back of the chapter.

A Costing

August 2018 – Variant 1 – task 2

> *I can compare different costing methods and systems to determine the most suitable for use by the organisation for different purposes*

[Trigger]

You arrive at work and read an announcement on the staff intranet that says that a new range of fruit-based infusions has been developed. There will initially be five new flavours.

Market research indicates that there is likely to be good demand for all flavours of the new range of infusions. In total, six new direct production workers will be taken on as an additional shift will be needed on the existing infusions production line. Fixed production overheads are expected to increase by D$400,000 annually as a result of this extra shift.

[Task]

Jack Ford, Head of Finance sends you the following email:

From:	Jack Ford, Head of Finance
To:	Finance Officer
Subject:	New range of infusions: costings

I've been working with Steve Gomez, Head of Production, on some of the financial implications from expanding the infusions range of products.

Steve is keen to understand the impact of the new products on our product costings and individual product gross margins. I've therefore estimated revised costings for all infusion products using our normal fixed overhead absorption approach and an activity-based costing (ABC) approach. I produced a schedule yesterday comparing these costings on one of our existing range flavours (peppermint) and one of the new range flavours (peach & raspberry), see attached.

Steve has now come back to me with the following queries about my schedule:

1   Why the costings for both Peppermint and Peach & Raspberry are different when the ABC approach is applied and what are the reasons for this difference?

2   How suitable would it be to use ABC to establish costings for our black and green tea products?

I would like you to prepare a briefing note that I can send to Steve which addresses his two concerns

---

COSTINGS ON INFUSIONS PRODUCTION LINE [Reference Material]

Peppermint Infusion (existing range)

Per box (D$)	Based on absorption costing using direct labour hours	Based on ABC
Contribution	0.72	0.72
Fixed production overhead	(0.11)	(0.09)
Gross profit	**0.61**	**0.63**
Gross margin	34.9%	36.0%

Peach & Raspberry Infusion (new range)

Per box (D$)	Based on absorption costing using direct labour hours	Based on ABC
Contribution	0.73	0.73
Fixed production overhead	(0.14)	(0.18)
Gross profit	**0.59**	**0.55**
Gross margin	33.7%	31.4%

Notes:

- The new range of infusions are to be produced in batches of 4,000kg of input. The new range infusion bags are a different shape to the existing range.

- For the new range a production run of a particular flavour will consist of two batches (compared to eight batches for each flavour of the existing infusion flavours)

- Before a production run can commence the blending drums and the production line need to be cleaned and dried to ensure the purity of the blend. The machinery that creates the bags also needs to be reset depending on the bag shape required for the next production run.

- The new range has an average of 10 different raw material inputs compared to an average of five for the existing range.

- Because the new range will have strings and tags attached to each bag, a greater number of quality checks will be required for each batch of production compared to the existing range to ensure quality.

Exercise 1

Prepare the briefing notes requested by Jack Ford

B Budgeting

August 2018 – Variant 4 – task 1

> *I can explain to functional managers how budgets are used for planning and control purposes.*

[Trigger]

The Research and Development (R&D) Department are working on a number of projects for new products as Thomas Fine teas seeks to expand its market share. One project, which is well advanced, is to develop a new tea bag design to be used for both green tea blends. The aim of the project is to design a tea bag which enables faster brewing and enriches the already luxurious taste of green tea. To this end the R&D team have been working closely with the tea bag paper supplier on a new type of paper and experimenting with the shape and content of the tea bag.

[Task]

You arrive at work and find the following email from Jack Ford:

From:	Jack Ford, Head of Finance
To:	Finance Officer
Subject:	New tea bag design for green tea

I have just been talking to Petra Dax, Head of R&D, about the green tea bag development project. She told me about a small-scale consumer trial that they have just done, and customer feedback is that the new tea bag enhances the flavour of the green tea. Until this trial, there were no firm plans to launch the new design into the market, as we don't know how the market would react, however we now plan to launch the new tea bag for our green tea blends with a marketing campaign emphasising the enhanced brewing quality due to its new design.

So far, we haven't revised the budget to include the impact of nationally launching this new tea bag design, partly because the potential impact on our sales of green tea is unknown and partly because Christie Smith, Finance Director, and I have been thinking about changing the business' approach to budgetary control. Christie's view is that it would be beneficial to use a feedforward control approach rather than a feedback control approach and is going to suggest to the rest of the senior management team that we start doing this with the green tea product range first.

I would like you draft the content for the briefing notes which explains how a feedforward control approach differs from a feedback control system. Please also explain the benefits to our business of using a feedforward control approach.

Exercise 2

Prepare the briefing notes requested by Jack Ford

August 2018 – Variant 5 – task 2

> *I can explain and use different forecasting methods to assist in budget preparation.*

[Trigger]

Thomas Fine Teas has agreed to purchase Butler Estates, a company based in Deeland that grows and sells unblended loose-leaf tea.

[Task]

Jack Ford, Head of Finance sends you the following email:

From:	**Jack Ford, Head of Finance**
To:	**Finance Officer**
Subject:	**Butler Estates**

I had a quick meeting with the directors yesterday and have been tasked with writing briefing notes on an issue that came up about Butler Estates.

The issue relates to how we go about forecasting medium term sales for Butler Estates, as there are currently no projections. As a result of our contacts we expect to expand the customer base but given we aren't involved in the loose tea business we need to consider how this market has been performing. Ben Jones, Sales & Marketing Director stated at the meeting that he has been able to get hold of some information from the Deeland Tea Organisation that shows the total sales of premium unblended loose-leaf teas for each quarter of the last five years in Deeland. He has suggested that we use this, together with other information, to create a time series. Other than Christie, the other directors were unsure about what a time series is and have asked me to send them some information on it. I've attached a recent article about Butler Estates which I'm sure you've seen before, hopefully this will help you.

I need you to prepare content for the briefing notes which explains how we can use the information obtained by Ben Jones to:

- Establish the trend and seasonal variations in a time series

- Explain what we might expect the trend and seasonal variation to show about sales of premium unblended loose-leaf tea

- Explain the appropriateness of this approach for forecasting Butler Estates sales

[Attachment]

TEA INDUSTRY GAZETTE

Butler Estates wins new contract

By: Rita Oolong

Deeland's only tea plantation, Butler Estates, has just won a major contract to supply Deeland's top department store with its high-quality 'Butler Tea' brand. This follows on from winning a prestigious tea award and adds to its growing customer base.

Butler Estates was established in 1996 in the southern tip of Deeland (the only part of the country with the correct climate for tea growing) by two brothers: Paul and Gareth Butler. The business does everything: grows the tea, harvests the tea, processes the tea into tea leaves and then packages as unblended loose-leaf tea, all on a single site.

The Butler brothers have taken advantage of increasing consumer demand in Deeland for quality unblended loose-leaf teas. The black tea 'Butler Tea' brand and the green tea 'Greener Blend' can now be found in high end delicatessens and food shops throughout Deeland. The business is at its busiest in spring and summer, although Gareth Butler comments that there is always plenty to do in the quieter months.

The teas produced by Butler Estates have won industry acclaim for their clarity of flavour, the high level of antioxidants which are retained from careful processing and a refreshing quality to the brew, especially in warm weather.

Butler Estates looks set to be one of Deeland's great entrepreneurial success stories as the only producer of home grown tea and I'm sure big things are ahead!

Exercise 3

Prepare the briefing notes requested by Jack Ford

C   Analysing performance

August 2018 – Variant 1 – task 4

I can interpret variances to review functional and organisational performance

[Trigger]

Thomas Fine Teas has developed a new range of fruit-based infusions. Initially these were produced by working additional shifts on the existing production lines but on the 1st January the decision was made to invest in a new production line. This became fully operational on the 1st April when the old production line reverted to just producing the original infusion flavours.

[Task]

Jack Ford, Head of Finance calls you and says:

There is a management meeting later this week, where we're going to discuss the variance report for April 2019, so I need you to prepare the following.

Could you prepare a commentary on the fixed production overhead variances for the infusions production line to include an explanation of what each variance means and the reasons for each variance. Please could you also include a brief explanation of the suitability of our fixed production overhead rates being based on direct labour hours? I've included the relevant variances on a schedule that you can come and collect from my office shortly.

I know there were a few issues with the new production line during April: it kept getting jammed in the first three weeks of production, although it now seems to be operating better since the installers came back to re-tune it. Due to this problem we have signed a 12 month maintenance contract for the line and paid 50% of the fee up front. Despite the jamming issues, I know that Steve is really pleased with the new line because when it is working properly the rate that the bags can be produced is significantly faster than he expected, although the machine ended up being more expensive than we originally budgeted for the year to 31March 2020.

You then go into Jack's office and pick up the variances schedule.

[Reference Materials]

FIXED PRODUCTION OVERHEAD VARIANCES FOR THE INFUSIONS PRODUCTION LINES FOR APRIL 2019

Fixed production overhead variances (Notes 1 and 2)	D$	Adv/Fav
Expenditure	97,875	Adverse
Efficiency	9,104	Favourable
Capacity	13,005	Favourable

Notes

1   We budgeted to produce 89 batches of infusions across both production lines in April 2019 but actually produced 95 batches.

2   The standards are those set for the budget for the year to 31 March 2020 and are based on fixed overhead costs for both infusion production lines and the total number of direct labour hours for infusions production

Exercise 4
Write your response to Jack Ford's requests.

D   Apply relevant financial reporting standards and corporate governance, ethical and tax principles.

Given the significant changes to the F1 syllabus, none of the tasks in the August 18 exam variants would be applicable under the 2019 syllabus.

Suitable examples are given in section 4 below.

E   Short-term decision-making.

August 20181 – Variant 1 – task 3

> *I can identify relevant costs and benefits.*

[Trigger]

Thomas Fine Teas has developed a new range of fruit-based infusions. Initially these were produced by working additional shifts on the existing production lines but sales have been so promising that four additional new flavours have been added to the range and, on the 1st January, the decision was made to invest in a new production line.

[Task]

Jack Ford, Head of Finance calls you into his office and says:

> 'I need you to do something for me.
>
> We are going to start producing the new flavours very soon, although the new production line is not going to be ready for three months which means that we will need to use the existing production line for all 12 flavours in the short term. The problem is that we do not have enough capacity to make all infusion products that we could sell in the three months before the new line is operational.
>
> Steve Gomez has been investigating various options to expand capacity until the new line is ready and has come up with a proposal.
>
> This involves hiring additional machinery from an external party, using a spare blending drum that is currently surplus to requirements on the black tea production line and temporarily transferring employees from the green tea production line to meet demand.
>
> Steve has just given me a list of what he thinks are the financial impacts of his proposal. Please let me know how each item on Steve's list will affect our evaluation of whether his proposal will be financially beneficial on a relevant costing basis. Please include any assumptions that you make about whether a cost is relevant.'

[Reference Material]

Steve Gomez Proposal

	D$'000
Cost of hiring and installing machinery from the external party (this includes a deposit of D$10,000 as a non-refundable holding fee, which has already been paid).	500
Net book value (NBV) of the blending drum. This drum is surplus to requirements and is due to be sold for D$50,000. If we use the drum for infusions, then we will lose the sale.	25
Gross profit (based on budgeted gross profit per box of infusions) from the additional sales generated from increasing capacity.	630
Cost of staff temporarily transferred from green tea production line.	28
Additional costs: insurance premium in respect of the hired machinery plus additional energy costs to run the hired machinery.	36
Cost of production manager's time supervising the installation of the hired machinery and blending drum.	3

Exercise 5

Write an email to Jack Ford in response to his requests

August 2018 – Variant 2 – task 1

I can apply appropriate techniques that support short-term decision-making.

[Trigger]

You have just had a week's vacation and read the following in an on-line newsfeed or your way to work in the morning:

Virulent disease affecting tea crops in Kenya:

An infectious disease is sweeping across the south of Kenya destroying tea crops. So far there have been no reports of the disease at tea plantations in the north of Kenya or other major tea growing countries. Quarantine restrictions are now in place in southern Kenya in a bid to halt the spread of the disease. Tea blenders in Deeland have already seen increases in the price of tea leaves and it looks like our morning cup of tea could soon be a little more expensive!

[Task]

At work Jack Ford, Head of Finance, calls you into his office and says:

'Hope you had a good week on vacation. Whilst you've been away a potential crisis has been developing with our tea leaf suppliers from Kenya due to the disease that has been reducing crop harvests. So far, we have established from our tea leaf dealers in Kenya, that three of the types of tea leaves used in our Everyday and Stronger blends are limited in supply. Our dealers are struggling to obtain supplies from the tea factories because those factories are prioritising supply to tea blenders with whom they have a direct relationship.

At the end of last week one of your colleagues prepared a linear programming graph to help establish how many batches of Everyday Blend and Stronger Blend should be produced in the next month. The graph includes constraints for each type of tea leaf which is in limited supply and a constraint for minimum production of 11 batches of Everyday Blend (this is to satisfy committed orders).

We have a senior management meeting later today where we are going to be discussing next month's production. I need you to prepare a briefing paper which explains:

- The constraints on the linear programming graph

- Where the feasible region is

- What the optimal production plan for Everyday Blend and Stronger Blend is

- What the binding constraints are and how we would determine the maximum we should pay for additional supplies of any tea leaf that is a binding constraint.

Jack Ford then hands you a schedule showing the linear programming graph that he referred to. This can be found as part of the reference materials below.

 Exercise 6

Prepare the briefing paper requested by Jack Ford.

[Reference materials]

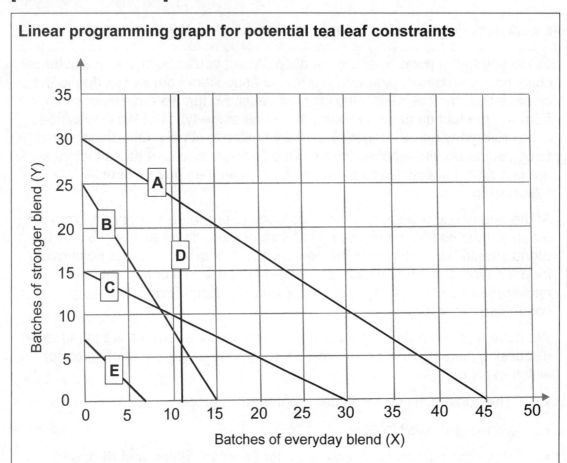

Linear programming graph for potential tea leaf constraints

Key for lines on the graph:

Line A: 1,200X + 1,800Y = 54,000 kg of leaf A

Line B: 2,800X + 1,680Y = 42,000 kg of leaf B

Line C: 1,200X + 2,400Y = 36,000 kg of leaf C

Line D: X = 11 batches of Everyday Blend

The objective is to maximise contribution and line E represents the iso-contribution line.

Note: It is possible, if necessary, to produce a partial batch of either Everyday blend or Stronger Blend.

F   Working capital management.

<u>August 2018 – Variant 1 – task 2</u>

> *I can explain how to manage and control working capital*

[Trigger]

You arrive at work and read an announcement on the staff intranet that says that a new range of fruit-based infusions has been developed. There will initially be five new flavours.

Market research indicates that there is likely to be good demand for all flavours of the new range of infusions. In total, six new direct production workers will be taken on as an additional shift will be needed on the existing infusions production line. Fixed production overheads are expected to increase by D$400,000 annually as a result of this extra shift.

[Task]

Jack Ford, Head of Finance sends you the following email:

From:	Jack Ford, Head of Finance
To:	Finance Officer
Subject:	New range of infusions: Inventory Management

I've been working with Steve Gomez, Head of Production, on some of the financial implications from expanding the infusions range of products.

Steve has asked me whether the Economic Order Quantity (EOQ) model might be a useful tool for managing inventory levels. Inventory management is going to be particularly important for the new range because there are so many different raw material inputs that need to be held, which is going to increase our inventory holding costs. There are various bulk discounts available and I know that Steve is keen to take advantage of these as far as possible.

I would like you to prepare a briefing note that I can send to Steve which explains what information we would need to calculate the economic order quantities for infusions raw materials and the appropriateness of using the EOQ model to manage the level of inventory held.

Jack Ford

Exercise 7
Prepare the briefing notes requested by Jack Ford

4 Examples of tasks from the February 2019 exam.

4.1 Summary of pre-seen scenario

As stated above, to fully appreciate examples from recent real exams it is necessary to have a basic understanding of the cases concerned.

The pre-seen information for February 2019 concerns a company called Trigg Adventures that designs, manufactures and installs children's outdoor play equipment in the country of Fawland.

Trigg offers high quality play equipment to both domestic and commercial customers.

Domestic products

Within the domestic sector Trigg is the recognised market leader, selling its products through specialist outdoor play stores, better toy shops and department stores and via its own website.

Unfortunately this market segment is mature with few growth prospects – recent growth has only averaged 1.7% per annum.

Commercial products

Higher growth is anticipated within the commercial sector with historic growth figures averaging 7.4%. Despite the best efforts of the previous MD, Trigg has yet to establish itself as a major player within this segment.

An article in the Fawland Business Today suggests that the key issue for commercial buyers is safety after several well publicised accidents in 2015. However, we are also told that Trigg's products adhere to all commercial safety standards ranking them at the highest level of safety in Fawland. Any deficiencies that customers perceive in Trigg must therefore be less about the products themselves but more about related issues such as installation.

One aspect of this could be previous problems encountered by Trigg, resulting in complaints, missed start dates and errors in installation. The decision to bring installation in-house rather than sub-contract has dramatically reduced such complaints but the company may still have to work hard to rebuild its reputation in this sector.

Another potential issue could be ground work. Instead of offering customers a one-stop solution in which Trigg sub-contracts ground work, customers are instead given recommendations concerning partner companies to do this aspect. This may be sufficient to make some look elsewhere.

Finally there have been problems in the past where employees with criminal records have ended up working at schools due to a lack of disclosure.

All of these issues must be addressed for Trigg to exploit enhanced future growth due to the government FITKIDS initiative.

Financial performance

Revenue fell by 4% from 2017 to 2018, resulting in a decrease of 15% in operating profit. This also reduced operating margins from 15.4% to 15.0%.

In terms of working capital and liquidity, cash increased by F$226,000 fuelled mainly by an increase in borrowing of F$300,000. It is questionable how future growth will be financed.

Inventory days and receivables days also increased resulting in an additional F$475,000 tied up in working capital.

The future

Budgeted sales for 2019 give an increase in revenue of 5% over 2018, which relies on increasing commercial sales.

This will depend very heavily on the extent to which Trigg can address the perceived weaknesses highlighted above and also whether Sally Gomez can use her previous experience at Jacks, a major competitor in the commercial sector, to increase Trigg's chances of winning commercial tenders.

4.2 Example tasks

As before, attempt each task before referring to the answers.

A Costing

February 2019 – Variant 5 – task 1

> I can compare different costing methods and systems to determine the most suitable for use by the organisation for different purposes

[Trigger]

Today is 1 March 2019. Yesterday the directors had a meeting where they discussed the future of the business and have agreed that, to grow, the business needs to increase its commercial market sales.

[Task]

You receive the following email from Ping Bennet, Finance Director

From:	Ping Bennet, Finance Director
To:	Finance Officer
Subject:	Commercial market: pricing

At yesterday's directors meeting, Sally Gomez, Sales Director, informed us that recently we have lost out to our competitors on a couple of commercial jobs that we tendered for and she believes that there are two main reasons for this.

Firstly our price wasn't competitive and secondly, when negotiating with the customers we focused solely on the quality of the climbing frames and failed to sell ourselves in respect of the high level of service that we would provide.

Clearly we need to address both of these matters to ensure that we can grow the commercial business.

I think part of the problem with pricing is because we use marginal costing: all jobs are priced on the basis of what we estimate our variable production and installation costs to be plus a 70% mark-up to cover overheads and our profit margin.

A mark-up of 20% is applied to accessories in recognition that less overhead is associated with these. I think we need to introduce a different costing approach and would like to investigate whether activity-based costing (ABC) might be appropriate across the business: for both domestic and commercial products. I have so far identified some activities related to the Stores Department and I have included two of these activities in an attachment to this email.

I would like you to prepare some notes for me which I can use to prepare a report to the other directors. I need your notes to explain the benefits of using absorption rather than marginal costing for pricing our commercial jobs. Please also explain if ABC would help with cost control and the issues we should consider when choosing cost drivers for activities identified on the attachment.

[Reference materials]

Attachment – Examples of stores activity

Activity	Detail
Ordering of accessories	Domestic products: accessories such as swings, slides and ropes are ordered in bulk to secure a bulk purchase discount. These accessories are kept in inventory to ensure that demand for domestic products can be satisfied quickly. The minimum order quantity for the bulk discount is 100 units of each item at a time.
	Commercial products: commercial jobs require larger scale and more durable accessories than those used for domestic products. Identical accessories are used in many commercial jobs but because of the size of some of these items, orders are usually made for five items each time.
Ordering of unique accessories	Because of the bespoke nature of commercial products, some commercial jobs require unique accessories that have to be sourced individually.
	When a unique accessory item is required the Design Team will inform the Stores Team, who will arrange for two quotes to be obtained from suppliers. Usually the cheapest quote is accepted.

Exercise 8

Write the notes requested by Ping Bennett

B   Budgeting

February 2019 – Variant 5 – task 2

> *I can compare alternative approaches to budgeting to determine their suitability for the organisation and for different purposes*

[Trigger]

Today is 1 March 2019. Yesterday the directors had a meeting where they discussed the future of the business and have agreed that, to grow, the business needs to increase its commercial market sales.

[Task]

Freddie Williams, Finance Manager, comes to your desk and says:

'I've just been speaking to Sally Gomez, Sales Director. She has asked for an increase in her Sales Department Budget given the drive to increase the customer base. In particular she would like to be able to attend more toy fairs to promote the brand because such events are usually well attended by retail buyers and commercial buyers alike. Ping Bennett, Finance Director, would like to introduce zero-based budgeting (ZBB) for support activities throughout the company and in view of Sally's request, she suggests that we should use this for the Sales Department, starting with the support activity of attending toy fairs. So that you understand the types of costs involved in attending toy fairs, I've prepared a list of actual expenditure for the last 12 months.

I will need to discuss this with Sally, so I would like you to prepare a briefing note which explains the steps involved in applying ZBB to establish budgets for support activities. Please illustrate your explanation using the support activity of attendance at toy fairs.'

[Reference materials]

Expenditure on Toy Fairs for the last 12 months

	F$000
Fees for attending three toy fairs (there were 15 toy fair events during the year throughout Fawland).	100
Travel and accommodation	12
Trade stand banners (usually replaced annually)	15
Promotional brochures given away	62
Free gifts (mugs, pens and key rings with company logo)	41

Exercise 9

Write the briefing note requested by Freddie Williams

C Analysing performance

February 2019 – Variant 2 – task 3

I can interpret variances to review functional and organisational performance

[Trigger]

In March the Directors decided to develop three new product ranges: climbing walls, playhouses and adventure platforms. The new ranges are indoor activity toys and are designed exclusively for businesses that use children's play equipment.

It is now early July and Freddie Williams, Finance Manager, is on leave. A new bonus scheme which applies to the climbing wall range, instead of the usual 0.5% bonus, has been in effect since the start of June. Under this scheme the sales team can earn F$10 per wall sold and have discretion to grant customers a discount of up to 15% to help boost sales for this new range.

[Task]

You receive the following email from Ping Bennett, Finance Director:

From:	**Ping Bennet, Finance Director**
To:	**Finance Officer**
Subject:	**Climbing wall sales variances and bonuses**

I have just spoken to Sally Gomez, Sales Director about the climbing wall sales variances that you sent her for June. She is concerned that while both the sales volume contribution variance and sales price variance are adverse, the sales team earned more bonus than budgeted. She asked me to check that the variances and bonus has been calculated correctly. I have checked both and they are correct.

To help Sally understand why this has occurred I have split the sales volume contribution variance into a sales quantity variance although I have not added commentary yet (see attached).

As Freddie is on leave, I need you to prepare briefing notes that I can send to Sally that give a detailed explanation of what the sales price, mix and volume variances indicate about the sales performance for the month and what effect the sales bonus scheme has had on these variances.

[Reference materials]

Selling price variances for climbing walls for June 2019

Product	Actual selling price (F$)	Budgeted selling price (F$)	Difference (F$)	Actual quantity sold (units)	Variance (F$)
Small climbing wall	510	600	(90)	75	(6,750)
Medium climbing wall	850	1,000	(150)	25	(3,750)
Large climbing wall	1,530	1,800	(270)	5	(1,350)
Total					(11,850)

Selling volume contribution, mix and quantity variances:

The sales volume contribution variance for the month of June is F$8,000 adverse. This has been subdivided into a favourable quantity variance of F$6,000 and an adverse mix variance of F$14,000. The following information is relevant:

Product	Actual quantity sold (units)	Actual quantity sold in budgeted mix (units)	Budgeted quantity sold (units)
Small climbing wall	75	35	30
Medium climbing wall	25	35	30
Large climbing wall	5	35	30
Total	105	105	90

Product	Budgeted contribution per unit (F$)	Actual contribution per unit (F$)
Small climbing wall	200	160
Medium climbing wall	400	320
Large climbing wall	600	480

Exercise 10

Write the briefing note requested by Ping Bennett.

D   Apply relevant financial reporting standards and corporate governance, ethical and tax principles.

<u>**February 2019 – Variant 4 – task 3**</u>

> *I can apply relevant IFRS in a given context, to facilitate the preparation of financial statements.*
>
> *I can identify the impact of tax regulation on transactions, decisions and profits.*

[Trigger]

In response to customer demands for sustainable products, a range of climbing frames using reclaimed timber and accessories made from recycled materials was developed and launched two months ago. So far the range includes two designs: Regular and Deluxe. The demand for this range is far exceeding expectations.

[Task]

You receive the following email from Freddie Williams, Finance Manager:

From:	**Freddie Williams, Finance Manager**
To:	**Finance Officer**
Subject:	**New Equipment**

We have invested in a new cutting machine: its purchase price was F$100,000, we spent F$5,000 having it installed and a further F$1,000 to have an independent inspection and certificate to ensure that we meet all health and safety requirements for this operation (this is a legal requirement). We also spent F$800 on bringing in an external training consultant to train the workers on its use. We expect this cutting machine to have a useful economic life of 10 years. We have also sold an old cutting machine for F$1,750. This had a tax written down value and a carrying value at the date of disposal of F$2,000.

Please email the following to me:

An explanation of

- Which elements of expenditure on the new cutting machine should be capitalised and which should not. Please use the criteria in IAS16: Property Plant and Equipment to justify your explanation.

- How the old cutting machine will affect this year's financial statements and the tax charge for the year

Exercise 11

Write your response to Freddie Williams.

E   Short-term decision-making.

February 2019 – Variant 2 – task 1

I can apply appropriate techniques to deal with situations where there is risk and uncertainty.

[Trigger]

Today is 1 March 2019. Grace Lucas, Design Manager, has led a project to develop three new product ranges: climbing walls, playhouses and adventure platforms. The new ranges are indoor activity toys and are designed exclusively for businesses that use children's play equipment.

[Task]

You receive the following email from Ping Bennett, Finance Director:

From:	**Ping Bennett, Finance Director**
To:	**Finance Officer**
Subject:	**New Products**

The senior management team have decided to launch one of the new product ranges immediately, with the intention of launching the other two in six months' time. We have a meeting tomorrow to choose which of the new product ranges to launch first.

We employed a consultant who confirmed on 14 January that the proposed market for the new product range was viable. The reaction of the market to each of the products is uncertain but the consultant has estimated the demand for each product in different market conditions. I have used those estimates to produce tables that show the payoffs and regrets. I've included these tables in an attachment to this email **[See reference materials below]**.

Please produce a briefing note for the next senior management meeting that explains the decision criteria we could use, based on the tables provided and given the uncertainty, to decide which of the new product ranges to launch first. Please also state the decision under each decision criterion.

Ping Bennett

Exercise 12

Write the briefing note requested by Ping Bennett.

[Reference materials]

Payoff and regret tables

The return expected from each product range in the first six months following launch:

Market demand	Climbing wall F$	Playhouse F$	Adventure platform F$
Low	40,800	108,000	32,400
Medium	129,600	141,000	124,800
High	218,400	174,000	256,800

Regret table:

Market demand	Climbing wall F$	Playhouse F$	Adventure platform F$
Low	67,200	0	75,600
Medium	11,400	0	16,200
High	38,400	82.800	0

F   Working capital management.

February 2019 – Variant 5 – task 2

I can explain how to manage and control working capital

[Trigger]

Today is 1 April 2019. Last month the directors had a meeting where they discussed the future of the business and agreed that, to grow, the business needed to increase its commercial market sales.

[Task]

Freddie Williams, Finance Manager, comes to your desk and says:

'I've just been speaking to Sally Gomez, Sales Director. She has requested that we extend the credit terms that we offer our commercial customers (except for local government customers). Currently we require these customers to pay on installation which effectively means they are not given any credit as this is the point we expect payment. Sally would like to offer 30 days after installation as the payment term because this would bring the commercial customer credit terms in line with smaller retailer customers for our domestic products.

> She thinks that we'll be able to win more commercial business this way. Obviously there will be implications of extending credit terms to these types of customer, but I suppose we could think about either factoring or introducing a prompt payment discount to deal with these. I've got a copy of the latest aged receivables report which I'll find for you in a moment.
>
> I will need to discuss this with Sally, so I would like you to prepare a briefing note which explains the implications of extending credit terms to commercial customers and the suitability of factoring or introducing a prompt payment discount in dealing with these implications.'

[Reference materials]

Aged Receivables report at 31 March 2019

	Total F$000	Current (within terms) F$000	0-30 days overdue F$000	30+ days overdue F$000
Domestic customers				
Large retailers	444	402	42	0
Small retailers	342	312	6	24
Total	**786**	**714**	**48**	**24**
Commercial customers				
Local Government	51	12	24	15
Other	30	0	30	0
Total	**81**	**12**	**54**	**15**

Exercise 13

Write the briefing note requested by Freddie Williams

5 Summary

Next steps:

(1) You can begin to revisit and revise technical material from your previous studies according to the core activities and assessment outcomes given in this chapter. However we suggest you continue to do this alongside working through the rest of this book so you can also learn how you may need to apply the knowledge.

(2) Remember that you are unlikely to have to perform calculations in the case study exam. However you may need to explain or interpret calculations and so an appreciation of how they are prepared is still relevant and useful.

(3) In the following chapters we do a complete walkthrough of the prototype sample paper issued in June 2019.

6 Solutions to chapter exercises

Exercise 1 (August 2018 variant 1 task 2)

BRIEFING NOTE

STEVE GOMEZ QUERIES ON INFUSION RANGE COSTINGS:

Why the costings are different and reasons for the difference:

With ABC, rather than a blanket overhead absorption rate being used to absorb overhead into product cost, overheads are divided into cost pools and those cost pools are absorbed into product cost based on a cost driver appropriate for that cost pool. A cost driver is the activity that drives or generates the cost.

Looking at the schedule, a greater share of the overhead cost is being absorbed by the new range when ABC is used. This is because the range is expected to generate more of the cost than a labour hour basis would indicate.

One reason for this is because the existing and new ranges have different production run sizes. After each production run the blending drum and line are cleaned and then the machinery is set up for the next production run. This activity generates cost each time it is performed and therefore it is appropriate for the products in the smaller production run to have a greater share of this cost.

Other reasons why the new range should take a greater share of the cost of activities are because the new range requires more quality checking during bag production as well as a greater number of raw materials movements.

The suitability of using ABC to establish product costings for black and green tea products:

Using ABC has many benefits: for example, a more meaningful product cost and a better indication of which activities drive costs ultimately leading to better cost control. Currently we use direct labour hours to absorb our overheads and whether we use ABC or not it is questionable whether this is an appropriate basis for us to use. Most of our production overheads (largely machinery running costs) are not driven by direct labour hours: under traditional costing it might actually be more appropriate to use machine hours.

ABC is costly to implement and hence it is important to weigh up this cost against the benefits. From the schedule we can see that the difference between the two bases of costing are relatively minor in respect of total product cost, which is because despite the differences in the production process between the existing and new range, by far the largest element of total cost is for raw materials. Any differences for our black and green tea ranges would be even smaller because for each of these, products are largely homogeneous.

However, production overheads for the business are significant and the mapping of production processes to understand what drives these costs would potentially allow us to start to reduce them. Indeed, this could be particularly beneficial for goods in, goods handling and despatch operations and therefore it could be worth considering implementing ABC on a wider scale.

Examiner's comments

Overall, this task was well done. In the first element, most candidates were able to explain the differences between ABC and traditional absorption costing and were then able to explain why this resulted in differences in the overhead costs for the infusion products. Weaker candidates were not able to clearly explain the connection between the differences in the two products (for example, the shape of the teabag) and the impact that this would have on the cost driver. However, most candidates gave good answers to this and scored well. The part of the requirement about ABC's suitability for black and green tea tended to be less applied and whilst candidates picked up a few marks for more generic points such as improved costing, pricing and cost control, they did not score as well as here.

Exercise 2 (August 2018 variant 4 task 1)

BRIEFING NOTES

FEEDFORWARD CONTROL

How a feedforward control approach differs from a feedback control system

Currently we use a feedback control system. We prepare our budgets based on our detailed knowledge of the business, compare these budgets to our actual results to calculate variances and feed this information back to the appropriate managers for action. This process forms part of the control loop: comparison to budget requires explanation, which looks towards either corrective action or a revision of the budget if the original budget is considered outdated for whatever reason.

Feedforward control involves the comparison of results that are currently forecast (given the latest information) with the planned results. Feedforward is a more positive system, in that it enables the anticipation of problems to prevent them from occurring. Essentially it compares the objectives for a future period (our desired expectations) with the actual results as they are now forecast. The essential principle of the feedforward control report is, as the description suggests, that it will look forward rather than back.

F or example, if we focus on the budgets for green tea, we will first need to establish the sales and production budgets based on what we initially expect to sell given the new tea bag design.

Under a feedback system, we wait until the end of a month to then compare this budget against the actuals to establish variances which are reported to the appropriate manager for action.

With a feedforward system, the process of feedback is much earlier. In the early stages of the month we can forecast what we expect to happen based on the latest information and compare this to the plan. Action can therefore be taken earlier.

Benefits to our business of using a feedforward control approach

The main benefit of using a feedforward system is that we can take corrective action much sooner. For example, if we have information from our marketing department that the new design is not selling as well as expected, we will need to take action to bring this back in line. This might be achieved with extended promotions, both for the retailers and customers, more instore advertising, and free trials. We need to create expectations regarding future performance identifying potential future issues for resolution.

The same will apply to the associated costs. Materials, labour and other overhead costs and cash requirements will have been established. Forecast changes in these must be monitored against the desired position. Excess material, labour usage and cash differences must be monitored, and differences highlighted so that action can be taken to rectify as soon as possible. For example, we might need to source tea leaves from other parts of the world if prices increase, or we might need to consider replacing machinery if the production output rate drops.

Certainly, for new projects such as expanding the infusions range or developing new tea blends, where there is a lack of established information, feedforward control appears worthwhile, and consideration should also be given to areas of the company such as cash forecasting where there is a constant necessity to look forward and update comparisons.

This will need to be balanced against the cost of providing updated forecasts when considering the more established elements of the business.

Examiner's comments

Answers in this task were mixed. Some candidates demonstrated little more than a basic understanding of feedforward control being forward looking and feedback control being backward looking, and others seemed confused and talked only about cash forecasting and rolling budgets. Other candidates wasted time discussing approaches to budgeting such as top down or zero-based budgeting, demonstrating perhaps a lack of technical understanding of feedback and feedforward control systems. Those that scored well here did so because they clearly demonstrated understanding of the different approaches with applied examples of the application of each.

Exercise 3 (August 2018 variant 5 task 2)

BRIEFING NOTES

TIME SERIES ANALYSIS

The Trend:

A series of trend data is established from the source data by calculating, at each quarter point in the period, an average of sales for the quarter based on the previous four quarters sales. This series of moving average can then then be plotted on a graph to establish the trend in sales over the five years. For premium unblended loose-leaf tea, we are likely to see an upward trend over the period as we know from industry and press reports that sales have grown for such products: consumers have become much more critical of food miles and are actively seeking to source local produce; they are also prepared to pay a premium price for this.

Seasonal variations:

Seasonal variations are fluctuations in or movements from the trend that are specific to a time of year. We will be able to identify this by comparing the moving average (which represents the trend) to actual demand at that point of the period. The variation will be seasonal if it reoccurs at the same point of time in each year. We will expect there to be seasonal variations in the summer and winter periods with higher sales in the summer and lower sales in the winter. This is because industry and press reports show that unblended teas are particularly popular with consumers when the weather is hot because they are more refreshing than standard tea.

Appropriateness of this approach:

This is potentially a sensible way in which to at least start to forecast future sales of Butler Estates teas because the source data is specifically for premium unblended loose-leaf teas (of which Butler Estates is one example). However, the following limitations need to be considered:

- The source data is historic and therefore it is entirely possible that what has happened in the past will not continue to happen in the future. The hot beverage market is highly competitive and new products such as infusions are being launched all the time which might affect demand for tea, even a premium branded tea.

- The source data is for the loose-leaf premium tea industry as a whole and hence will not take the specific characteristics of Butler Estates teas into account; that being the fact that it is the only tea grown in Deeland.

- Time series assumes that the trend can be established as a linear relationship between sales and time and that seasonal variations are proportional to the trend.

In reality a linear relationship might not exist, and it could be that cyclical or random factors (such as economic recession or an excessive hot summer) cause variations from trend which make it much harder to predict the future.

- There could be many factors which affect future demand for Butler Estates tea including competitors, health crazes and environmental changes.

Examiner's comments

Many candidates struggled with this task. Common problems were a failure to be able to explain how seasonal variations were calculated, and whether time series analysis would be appropriate. Regarding appropriateness, far too many candidates simply said that it would help with planning or budgeting. What was expected was a critical discussion of issues such as the past may not indicate the future, the influence of random variations and the assumption of linearity.

Exercise 4 (August 2018 variant 1 task 4)

FIXED PRODUCTION OVERHEAD VARIANCES FOR INFUSIONS

Expenditure variance D$97,875 adverse:

The expenditure variance is adverse which means that we incurred a higher level of overhead than we budgeted to in the month of April. One reason for this is that the machinery for the new line ended up costing more than we had anticipated which means that the depreciation charge within the fixed overhead will be higher than we originally budgeted. Additionally, because of the jamming problems we have taken out a 12-month maintenance contract that was not anticipated at the time the budget was prepared. This will be additional overhead cost. It's possible as well that the entire amount paid has been booked to overhead rather than spread over six months, therefore next month the impact will be less.

Efficiency variance D$9,104 favourable:

The efficiency variance is favourable which means that we used less direct labour hours to carry out actual production than we should have based on the standard. This is slightly surprising given the jamming problem which meant there were disruptions to production leading to downtime as well as direct production workers wasting time sorting out the jams: the impact of this would have led to an adverse variance. One reason for a favourable variance is because the rate of bag production on the new line is significantly better than anticipated which means that less direct labour time was required per batch than we planned. The standards for direct labour hours should be re-assessed based on the operation of the new line. It is also possible that the old line was more efficient than expected having reverted back to handling only three different flavours.

Capacity variance D$13,005 favourable:

The capacity variance is favourable which means that actual direct labour hours worked were higher than we had originally budgeted. This is because of producing more batches than anticipated because of the higher rate of bag production on the new line. The capacity of our production lines is higher than we expected.

Suitability of fixed production overhead absorption rate being based on direct labour hours:

From our standard cost cards, we can see that fixed production overhead is a significant proportion of the total cost of producing a batch of each product (it accounts for roughly 25% of the total cost of a batch of infusion). However, we can also see that the cost of direct labour is a relatively small proportion (roughly 2% of the total cost of a batch of infusion).

Fixed production overhead costs largely consist of the fixed costs of running our production machinery (such as depreciation and maintenance costs) and are relatively high because our production processes are highly mechanised. This is also the reason why our direct labour hours are relatively low: because of mechanisation we do not need input from direct production workers.

Our fixed production overheads costs (mostly machinery running costs) largely arise because the production machinery is operating, rather than because of direct labour input.

Therefore, a more suitable basis for absorbing fixed production overhead would be machine hours rather than direct labour hours.

Examiner's comments

The variance analysis element of the task produced a mixed quality of answers. Many candidates had a clear understanding of the fixed overhead expenditure variance, fewer candidates were quite so clear when explaining the efficiency and capacity variances. Some candidates thought it would be enough to restate the issues in the scenario which would have affected performance and made no attempt to separately explain the efficiency and the capacity variance or to identify each of the issues with the individual variances. Most candidates were able to comment on the reasons why direct labour hours was not the best basis for overhead absorption and why machine hours were better.

Exercise 5 (August 2018 variant 1 task 3)

FINANCIAL VIABILITY OF HIRING ADDITIONAL PRODUCTION MACHINERY

To assess the financial viability of Steve Gomez's solution we need to establish the net incremental financial effect on a relevant costing basis. If the effect is a net financial benefit, then it is worthwhile and if it is a net financial loss, then it is not worthwhile.

Relevant costs and revenues are those which are incremental (that is only arise as a result of the decision), future (that is are yet to happen) and ultimately result in cash flows for the business.

Cost of hiring and installing the machinery:

Most of the D$500,000 is a relevant cost of the decision because it will only be incurred if we decide to hire the machinery.

The only bit that isn't relevant is the D$10,000 deposit which has already been paid: this is a sunk cost (in the past) and not relevant.

Blending drum:

The net book value of the blending drum is not relevant as this is an accounting value based on past historical cost.

However, there is an opportunity cost here because if the drum is used for infusions we will lose the sale proceeds. Thus, D$50,000 is the value that needs to be treated as a cost of the decision.

Gross profit on additional sales:

Standard gross profit per box is calculated as revenue less total production costs which includes both direct costs as well as variable and fixed overheads. The latter needs to be excluded as the fixed overhead should not change with the level of output.

Instead of gross profit, contribution per box should be used to calculate the net cash inflow from the additional sales.

Temporary transfer of staff:

The cost of the staff that are temporarily transferred is likely to be not relevant on the basis that the wages are probably a committed cost. However, we need to consider whether there are any opportunity costs arising from these staff being transferred. Will green tea production and sales suffer as a result of the transfer?

We also need to consider if there are any additional costs for training or any overtime premiums required which would be relevant.

Additional costs:

The additional costs should be included because these are incremental and only occur because of the decision.

Production managers time:

The value of production managers' time to supervise installation should not be included in the evaluation of this decision because production managers' salaries are a committed cost. We will have to pay them irrespective of whether they undertake this supervision. Therefore, this should be excluded.

Examiner's comments

This task was generally well answered, although most failed to recognise that the fixed overhead element of gross profit was not relevant. Some candidates didn't actually explain why some of the costs were relevant or not relevant and were therefore not awarded the marks. A number also tried to work out a revised costing at the end which was not required and would have wasted time. Others also discussed non-financial factors, which has been asked for in this type of question in the past but was not required on this occasion and therefore gained no credit.

Exercise 6 (August 2018 variant 2 task 1)

BRIEFING PAPER

Constraints and feasible region:

Line A on the graph represents different combinations of production of Everyday Blend and Stronger Blend that will utilise all of the 54,000 kilogrammes of Leaf A that are available.

Lines B and C represent the same for tea leaves B and C. Line D on the graph represents the committed orders of 11 batches of Everyday Blend; this is the minimum level of Everyday Blend that needs to happen.

To find the optimal production plan we need to look at the constraint lines together. We do this by defining the feasible region for production which will be the area below the tea leaf constraint lines A, B and C and to the right of the minimum production constraint line D.

From the graph, the feasible region is the triangle which is to the right of line D, underneath constraint line B and above the X axis.

Optimal production plan for Everyday Blend and Stronger Blend:

Having defined the feasible area, the optimal solution is found by moving the iso-contribution line (Line E) as far from the origin as possible, because this is the point at which contribution will be maximised.

The optimal production plan is to produce 11 batches of Everyday Blend and approximately 6.5 batches of Stronger Blend.

This is at the point where lines B and D cross.

Binding constraints and what to pay for additional tea leaves:

Based on an optimal production plan of 11 batches of Everyday Blend and 6.5 batches of Stronger Blend, the binding constraints are the minimum level of production of Everyday Blend (Line D) and tea leaf B (line B).

The maximum price we should pay for additional supplies of tea leaf B will be the normal price per kilogramme plus the shadow price, where the shadow price is the increase in contribution from obtaining an extra kg of tea leaf B.

To calculate the shadow price for tea leaf B, the first step would be to use simultaneous equations to accurately establish the optimal solution if we had 42,000 kilogrammes and 42,001 kilogrammes of tea leaf B. We would then calculate the contribution generated from each of these optimal solutions; the difference would be the shadow price.

> **Examiner's comments**
>
> *Answers to this task were mixed. Many candidates were able to competently explain the constraints, feasible region and optimal solution, although a common error was to ignore the minimum production constraint for Everyday Blend which was a little disappointing. Most candidates however failed to address the final bullet point about the binding constraint: some added a few brief comments about shadow price but failed to explain what this meant and how it could be determined. There appeared to be a lack of technical understanding here.*

Exercise 7 (August 2018 variant 1 task 2)

BRIEFING PAPER

INVENTORY MANAGEMENT

Information required to calculate EOQ:

For each type of infusions raw material (for example, paper, packaging, dried fruit, fruit and herbal leaves) we will need to establish:

- Annual demand which will be driven by the level of anticipated production.

- The cost of an individual order which will include procurement staff time, internal administrative costs and any goods in delivery costs.

- The cost of holding one unit of inventory for one year. Holding costs will include insurance, storage costs (including energy used in the warehouse, staff training costs for safe handling, handling staff time) and the finance cost associated with the investment in working capital.

The appropriateness of the EOQ model:

In principle, the EOQ model is useful because it would give us for each type of raw material inventory the order quantity which would minimise the overall cost of both ordering and holding that inventory. However, the EOQ model is based on assumptions which can make its practical application difficult.

The model assumes that demand for the raw material is constant throughout the year and can be determined with a reasonable level of certainty: both are unlikely for the infusions range. Despite positive market research there is still considerable uncertainty regarding how popular and successful the new range will be; there is also uncertainty over which flavours will be popular. Demand for the new infusions is likely to gradually grow through the year as more and more people hear about and try it.

It is assumed that the lead time is constant or zero, however for us it is possible that lead times will vary through the year, especially as a large portion of raw materials are plant- based and dependent upon harvests and crop yields. Both uncertainty in demand and variable lead times can be adjusted for in the EOQ model by setting a safety or buffer level of inventory. This increases overall holding costs but allows flexibility to schedule production where demand is higher than expected or where lead times are longer than expected. The downside though of holding safety inventory is that the risk of obsolescence increases (especially for the plant-based materials).

The model also assumes that purchase costs are constant with no bulk discounts and that holding costs are variable with the level of inventory held. The former of these assumptions can be dealt with by expanding the analysis to consider the inventory level that minimises the total of holding, ordering and net of discount purchase costs. The latter assumption is more difficult to justify because in reality a significant portion of holding costs such as the costs of operating the warehouse are fixed in nature.

In conclusion, the EOQ model is not going to be wholly appropriate to use on a practical level. This is because of the uncertainty of future demand and because of the nature of our inventory. However, it could be used as a guide with practical factors such as shelf life of the plant-based materials taken into account.

Examiner's comments

This task was reasonably well answered. Most candidates were able to state the elements that went into the EOQ model, but few gave examples of the type of costs which would constitute holding and ordering costs. Some candidates gave very vague answers on the appropriateness of EOQ and failed to question the appropriateness of whether the assumptions underpinning the model (such as constant and known demand) applied in this case.

Exercise 8 (February 2019 variant 5 task 1)

BRIEFING PAPER

ACTIVITY-BASED COSTING (ABC)

Implication of using a full costing approach rather than marginal costing on pricing

Under marginal costing fixed overheads are ignored when establishing the unit costs for our domestic products and the costs associated with commercial jobs. As a result, we do not know the full cost of our products and therefore pricing is potentially an issue.

In the longer term, to be a profitable business we need to ensure that all costs are covered by the selling prices we achieve: if we do not know the full cost of say a domestic climbing frame we cannot be sure that this will be achieved. Including an appropriate share of production overhead will allow us to establish the total cost to make our products and gives us a base against which we can compare the prices that we are able to achieve in the market. This will give us more accurate information about the relative profitability of our products.

This is particularly acute in relation to commercial jobs where we currently add a 70% margin onto the variable costs of production and installation to arrive at selling price. This is an arbitrary and significant margin and could mean that we either under-price or over-price when giving a quote: recent feedback from Sally would indicate that we are actually over-pricing and that this margin is potentially too high.

Implication of using ABC on cost control

ABC works on the basis that the activities that generate cost are identified and production overhead is split into cost pools that relate to these activities. The act of identifying the activities gives us detailed information about why production overheads arise and by knowing this we are more able to control these costs. For example, with purchasing, the order size for accessories used regularly on commercial jobs is considerably smaller than for domestic products (5 compared to 100). Each order made generates cost to the business and therefore it might actually be more cost effective to increase the order size, although we would of course have to factor in the additional cost of holding inventory. The point is though, that ABC makes us look in detail at what drives overhead and gives us information to allow change for better cost control.

Issues to consider when determining cost drivers for the purchasing of accessories

To determine the cost driver for accessories in regular use we need to consider what causes cost to be incurred. For such items each time an order is placed a cost will arise (predominately staff time) and thus the cost driver will be the number of orders for each type of accessory (domestic or commercial).

The order size for commercial jobs is far smaller than for domestic products and therefore it would be appropriate that commercial jobs would receive a greater share of the costs associated with purchasing accessories in regular use.

To determine the cost driver for unique accessories we also need to consider what causes cost to be incurred. Each unique accessory requires two quotes to be obtained which will generate a cost and presumably the cost will be the same or very similar for each unique accessory required. Therefore, the driver of the cost will be the number of unique accessories ordered and under ABC, each time the sale team place an order for a unique accessory they will be aware of the cost implications associated.

Examiner's comments

This task was largely answered well from a technical point of view. Most candidates were able to recognise that the key difference between using the full costing approach instead of the marginal costing approach is the treatment of fixed production overhead. Similarly, most were able to discuss the implications for cost control of using activity-based costing (ABC) rather than marginal costing and most attempted to link this to cost drivers. However, many candidates fell short of taking the final step of applying this theory to different types of accessories referred to in the scenario. Few were able to link the cost drivers to be the number of orders and explore how this applied to Trigg Adventure to gain the full marks available here.

Exercise 9 (February 2019 variant 5 task 2)

BRIEFING PAPER

APPLICATION OF ZERO-BASED BUDGETING TO SALES DEPARTMENT BUDGET

Establish activities and objectives

The first stage of the process will be to decide on the decision units: effectively the support activities within each department that will generate cost. Each activity will have an objective associated with it. For example, the objective of attending toy fairs is to generate new business and create a buzz about the products.

Establish decision packages

For each activity, there will be potentially different ways in which its objective can be achieved or different levels of expenditure that could be incurred. These choices are reflected in decision packages which should be drawn up by those people closest to the activities (that is the sales people rather than the finance team). Decision packages can either be mutually exclusive (different ways of achieving the objective) or incremental (different levels of service to achieve slightly different outcomes).

There are many toy fairs across the country and currently we only attend a small number each year. We could create decision packages for individual toy fairs (each with different attendance fees and travel / accommodation costs and different potential benefits in terms of the likely attendees). Each of the toy fairs attended would potentially achieve the same objective, although perhaps with different degrees of success.

Creating a decision package for each will allow us to compare and to select the toy fairs that would potentially be most beneficial.

Incremental decision packages can also be developed for each toy fair. We could start with a base package where maybe there are no free gifts and the brochures used are simple (perhaps black and white and giving only basic information). This is potentially a risky strategy given the competitive nature of the commercial market, and the fact that we want to increase market share: customers will expect glossy brochures and if our competitors are giving away free gifts, we will need to as well. Therefore, we need to develop packages that incrementally increase the level of spend in terms of free gifts and brochures. For each package we would need to establish the anticipated cost of the marketing and the benefits to be derived in terms of additional business and contribution into the business.

Perform cost/benefit analysis and rank decision packages

Once the decision packages have been fully developed, a cost/benefit analysis needs to be performed. Clearly, the main benefit of attending toy fairs is to generate interest in our products and to grow sales. There are other benefits though in terms of keeping up to date with what our competitors are doing and seeing what the latest trends are in respect of outdoor toys. Each decision package would need to be considered against these benefits and then ranked in order of preference.

Allocate resources

Once all decision packages across the business for support activities such as the Sales Department have been ranked the whole budget would need to be considered and the resources available allocated to each part of the business accordingly.

Examiner's comments

Answers for this task were mixed. Most candidates were able to explain the basic approach of zero-based budgeting, but didn't extend that to include decision units, or explore the objectives of the activity, such as being able to generate new business and raising brand awareness. Some were able to link their answer to considering the cost-benefit aspects of support activities, but most discussed the individual costs of attending the toy fairs rather than exploring decision packages and the potential ranking of the most effective activities. This limited application meant that most candidates couldn't score highly in this task.

Exercise 10 (February 2019 variant 2 task 3)

SALES VARIANCES

Sales price variance F$11,850 adverse

This variance shows that the actual selling price achieved was less than the budgeted selling price for all three products in the range. The sales team were given the discretion to offer customers a discount in order to secure a sale and the difference between the actual and budgeted selling price indicates that this discount was offered freely. The motivation for the sales staff offering the discount is probably due to the fact that their bonus was based on units sold and not on achieving the budgeted selling price.

Sales mix variance F$14,000 adverse

The sales mix variance indicates the increase or decrease in profit due to the actual total volume of products being sold in a different proportion to the budgeted mix. We must have sold proportionately more of the lower contribution products and less of the higher contribution products to achieve this adverse variance.

As can be seen from the data we have sold significantly more of the small climbing walls than the actual quantity in the budgeted mix and these products have the lowest standard contribution of all the items sold. Similarly, we can see that we sold significantly less than the actual quantity in budgeted mix of the large climbing walls and these items are the items with the highest standard contribution. It is probable that these differences in product sales have been influenced by the bonus scheme. As the bonus is paid at a flat rate per item, regardless of the type of item, it is likely that the sales team have focused on selling the smaller climbing walls because they are easier to sell. This could be because they are less of a financial outlay.

Sales quantity variance F$6,000 favourable

The sales quantity variance quantifies the effect on our contribution of selling a higher quantity in standard mix than budgeted. We sold 105 climbing walls which is more than the 90 budgeted and when this difference is multiplied by the standard contribution it indicates that we have earned F$6,000 more contribution than budgeted.

The reasons for this variance are not altogether clear. However, as the sales team are paid a bonus for each item sold, it is possible that the bonus has motivated them. Another reason for the variance could be because this is the first month of sales of the climbing walls and that the forecasts could have been inaccurate, so it follows that our sales budgets are inaccurate.

Sales volume contribution variance F$8,000 adverse

The sales volume variance is the sum of the sales mix and sales quantity variances. It quantifies the effect on our contribution due to selling 105 units rather than the budgeted 90 units.

This variance is adverse overall because the positive effect on contribution gained from the quantity does not overcome the negative effect on contribution caused by the sales mix variance.

Examiner's comments

Answers for the second element of this task were on the whole very good. Sales variances have been examined many times and it is evident to me that candidates find it easier to talk about sales mix and quantity variances compared to the raw materials or labour equivalent.

Most candidates were able to explain what each of the variances meant, how they might have arisen and the impact that the bonus scheme had.

Exercise 11 (February 2019 variant 4 task 3)

NON-CURRENT ASSETS

Purchase of new equipment

To capitalise expenditure as part of plant and equipment we must be sure that a tangible non-current asset has been created.

Under IAS 16: Property, plant and equipment, the two criteria to recognise an asset are that it is probable that the asset will generate future economic benefit (this is met because the cutting machine has been purchased to facilitate production) and is capable of reliable measurement (this is met because we know how much we spent on it). In addition, the asset must be a physical asset (which it is) and expected to be used for more than 12 months (it has a useful economic life in the business of 10 years).

The amount that can be capitalised will be the total of the assets purchase price (F$100,000) and any expenditure directly attributable to getting the asset ready for its intended use. The first item of expenditure which is directly attributable is the F$5,000 spent on installation. The cutting machine could not have been used without being properly installed and therefore this is directly attributable to getting it ready for its intended use. The second item of expenditure which is directly attributable is the F$1,000 spent on the Health and Safety inspection and certificate. It is a legal requirement to have this and therefore is a cost of getting the asset ready for its intended use: without the certificate the cutting machine could not legally be used.

The only item of expenditure that cannot be capitalised is the F$800 spent on training. The cutting machine will have been ready for its intended use whether or not the staff are trained. In addition, training is associated with people, who are free to leave employment and take the knowledge from the training with them. As a result, expenditure on training is not capitalised.

Disposal of old equipment

We will need to record the disposal of the old cutting machine in the financial statements. There will be a loss on disposal of F$1,750 – F$2,000 recorded in the statement of profit or loss, which will have the effect of reducing profit for the year. The value of property, plant and equipment will also be reduced by F$2,000 in the statement of financial position. The disposal proceeds of F$1,750 will also appear as an investing cash inflow in the statement of cash flows.

The old cutting machine will also need to be disposed of for tax purposes which will affect the corporate tax computation for the year. The tax charge for the year is based on taxable profit multiplied by the tax rate. Taxable profit is accounting profit plus non-allowable expenses such as depreciation and less allowable expenses such as tax depreciation allowances.

The disposal will affect the tax depreciation allowances for the year: there will be a balancing allowance of F$2,500 – F$1,750 which will increase the value of tax depreciation allowances and lower the tax charge

Examiner's comments

Most candidates understood the principles of IAS16 and were able to apply these principles to the facts provided to them in the task and as a result, earned the full, or nearly full, marks available for this part. The part of the task asking candidates to explain how the old machine would be treated in the financial statements and for tax purposes was less well answered.

Not many candidates discussed statement of financial position or statement of cash flow implication of the disposal, and many candidates were confused about how the asset disposal would be treated for tax purposes.

Exercise 12 (February 2019 variant 2 task 1)

DECISION CRITERIA UNDER CONDITIONS OF UNCERTAINTY

The three decision criteria used under conditions of uncertainty are known as maximax, maximin and minimax regret.

Maximax criterion

A decision maker that uses the maximax criterion is an optimist. Using this approach, the option chosen will be the one that offers the maximum monthly return. The maximum return here for each product range are: F$218,400 for the climbing wall, F$174,000 for the playhouse and F$256,800 for the adventure platform.

Therefore, under this criterion we will choose the adventure platform as this gives us the highest possible return.

Maximin criterion

A decision maker that uses the maximin criterion is a pessimist. Using this approach, the range that maximises the minimum return achievable will be selected. The minimum returns for each of the three ranges are: F$40,800 for the climbing wall, F$108,000 for the playhouse and F$32,400 for the adventure platform.

Therefore, under this criterion we will choose the playhouse as this is the highest of the three lowest returns.

Minimax regret criterion

A decision maker that uses the minimax regret criterion is often referred to as a "bad loser". The decision is made by firstly identifying the product range that maximises the return at each of the three market conditions. The differential between the highest return and the other two at each of the market conditions represents the regret of having made a bad choice.

If the market demand is low the playhouse has the best return and so the regret of choosing the playhouse is F$0. The climbing wall has a regret of F$67,200 (= F$108,000-F$40,800) and the adventure platform has a regret of F$75,600 (= F$108,000-F$32,400).

Once we have completed the regret table we then choose the product range that minimises the maximum regret, or to put it another way, we select the best of the worst. So, the maximum regrets for each product range are: F$67,200 for the climbing wall, F$82,800 for the playhouse and F$75,600 for the adventure platform.

Therefore, under this criterion we will choose the climbing wall as this has the minimum of the maximum regrets of the three product ranges.

Examiner's comments

Most candidates were able to answer this task well and were able to explain the difference between maximax and maximin, although fewer were able to explain minimax regret.

Many candidates were able to correctly apply the methods to the data given and identify the decision under each of the criteria.

Exercise 13 (February 2019 variant 5 task 2)

EXTENDING CREDIT TERMS

Implications of extending credit terms

The first implication of extending credit terms to commercial customers is that our receivables days will increase which in turn will increase the length of the operating cycle. This means that more money will be tied up in working capital, which either needs to be financed via an overdraft or results in less money available for us to pay our suppliers and other commitments on time.

If we do not pay our suppliers on time this means, despite the good relationships we currently have, that we might start to develop poor relations with them. It also means that we might not be able to take advantage of any prompt payment or bulk purchase discounts available from our suppliers.

Another implication is that the risk of receivables balances ultimately not being paid is increased. The aged receivables report at 31 March 2019 shows that already our customers take longer to pay than they should, and this increases the risk that they will never pay. Whilst we can expect the local government to ultimately pay what is already overdue, for our domestic small retailers there is potentially an issue as F$24,000 is more than 30 days late. Clearly our credit controller will be dealing with this, but the risk of non-payment is likely to be higher with these smaller scale retailers because there is a higher chance of these types of customer ceasing to trade, compared to the larger retailers and local government.

Non-local government commercial customers are likely to be similar to our existing small retailer customers and therefore extending credit terms will increase the risk of irrecoverable debts.

Suitability of suggestions of how to manage implications

Factoring would involve a factoring business advancing us say 80% of the value of invoices as they are raised, and this means that we would receive a significant proportion of the monies due to us earlier than normal: this would help in managing cash-flow. A factor would also take over responsibility for managing the receivables ledger and because they are experts in credit control this means that it is likely they would recover more of the monies owed to us. We could even take out a 'without recourse' arrangement which would mean that the factor has responsibility for irrecoverable debts: this would eliminate our risk to irrecoverable debts.

However, factoring is expensive, and we would need to consider the cost of this against the benefits to cash flow and reduced risk.

Offering a prompt payment discount to all of our credit customers might encourage at least some of our customers to pay earlier than they would normally which means that cash comes into the business more quickly, however not all customers will take advantage of it.

It might also mean that some customers end up paying before they run into difficulties and the debt becomes irrecoverable, although this is likely to apply in only a small number of cases. Like with factoring we would need to consider the benefits to be gained against the cost of giving away the discount (which, at maybe 1% or 2% of invoice value, could be significant).

Examiner's comments

This task was reasonably well answered by most, although some candidates focused their answer on methods of verifying the creditworthiness of customers, which isn't what was asked for. Many candidates could appreciate that extending credit terms to customers had some advantages for Trigg Adventure. They were also able to highlight the practical implications to the business, such as the impact on cash flow and working capital by allowing customers to take longer to pay, and the increased risk of irrecoverable debts. The factoring and prompt payment parts to this task were answered very well overall, with many candidates scoring full marks here.

2019 Prototype exam – pre-seen information

Introduction

The Case Study Examinations are like no other CIMA exam; there is no new syllabus to study or formulae to learn. The best way to be successful at this level is to practise using past case study exams and mock exams based on your real live case study. By reviewing previous case studies alongside your current case you will improve your commercial thought processes and will be more aware of what the examiner expects. By sitting mock exams, under timed conditions you can hone your exam techniques and, in particular, your time management skills.

This textbook is therefore based on this principle. It presents the prototype case study and uses this to demonstrate the skills and techniques that you must master to be successful. The prototype case, GymFiT, will be used to walkthrough the processes and approach. The remainder of this chapter contains the GymFiT pre-seen material.

We would advise that you skim read this now before moving on to Chapter 4 where you will be provided with more guidance on how to familiarise yourself with the pre-seen material.

1   Extract from job description

You are a Finance Officer for GymFit. Your main role is to support Steven Potter, the Finance Manager. Your tasks include the production of the annual budget, producing the monthly management accounts and providing information to management as required. You also assist with the preparation of the financial statements and deal with any queries regarding financial reporting.

2   Company Information

GymFit, is a fast growing, leading provider of low-cost gyms and one of the pioneers of the low-cost gym model, which is based on relatively low gym membership fees and a 'no-frills' service concept. It now has 102 gyms with 486,000 members based in major towns and cities throughout Celtland, Europe. The company was founded in 2005 using finance from venture capitalist, Land Ventures. It is currently listed in the Celtland stock exchange and uses the C$ as its home currency.

Revenue 2013 – 2018 in $000

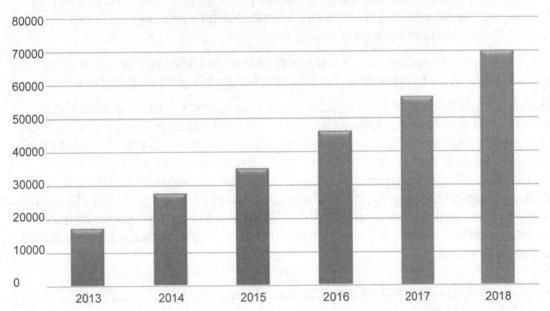

The company has grown rapidly from sales revenue of C$17.8 million in 2013 to C$73.1 million in 2018. The number of gyms it operates has also increased during the same period from 26 gyms to 102. The rapid increase in the number of gyms has been through a mixture of organic growth and acquisition of existing gym groups. The company is now the 2nd largest operator of low-cost gyms in Celtland.

GymFit's business model offers 24/7 gym operating hours and a no-contract membership i.e. there is no fixed membership period. The high specification gym equipment used is eco-friendly. In order to offer low membership fees, their model is based on a no-frills concept, meaning that facilities are restricted to the gym equipment, there are no wet facilities e.g. saunas or pools, and no café or bars that you would expect to find in a traditional health club.

The low-cost model used by GymFit is dependent on advanced technology. Prospective GymFit members can join using a simple online process that can be completed in minutes. Members can also manage their accounts, view class timetables and book classes online.

The use of technology results in an efficient staffing model with, for example, no need for dedicated in-gym sales and marketing teams.

Membership

GymFit membership is on a no-contract basis i.e. it does not involve a fixed membership period and members are free to cancel their membership at any time without penalty. There are three types of membership: solo gym membership, where the member is able to access only one chosen gym; two gym membership, where the member can access two chosen gyms and bundle membership where the member can access gyms nationwide. These types of membership require payment of a monthly fee. In addition, it is possible to access gym facilities on a daily basis by purchasing a day pass. Membership fees vary depending mainly on the location of the gym. Occasional marketing campaigns are run offering discounted membership to all new members. Student members also receive a discount.

Each member is provided with a unique personal identification number (PIN) code which is used to provide electronic access to the gym and its facilities.

Members have access to high quality fitness equipment, work-out areas and some free fitness classes. Other classes such as Pilates, yoga and dance fit are available on payment of an additional fee. All new members are offered a free induction session and these are provided by the fitness instructors. The member can also, on payment of an additional fee, arrange for individual coaching from a fitness instructor. These additional fees are paid directly to the instructors and are a private arrangement between the gym member and the instructor. Other facilities offered include showers, changing areas, lockers and vending machines.

The People

Staff

The average number of employees, during 2018, was 254. A typical gym has two employees, a manager and an assistant manager, who manage the running of the gym. The remaining staff are employed at head office in various functions including IT, HR, Finance and Marketing. These employees are complemented by a number of freelance fitness instructors who are hired on a zero-hours contract where the instructors are not guaranteed to be offered work in any one week. The fitness instructors are paid a relatively low hourly rate but are able to supplement their income with fees from individual coaching sessions.

All fitness instructors are trained fitness experts. Their main role is to assist members with using the equipment, run induction sessions for new members, lead some group classes, and provide general exercise and fitness advice. They are also expected to carry out simple preventative maintenance and testing the equipment. They can generally resolve most of the simple problems arising with the equipment, anything they cannot deal with is referred to the contracted maintenance company. In addition to this, they also refill vending and water machines and, where possible, attend additional training sessions related to equipment use, fitness or health and safety.

Gym managers are empowered to independently run their own sites, including the setting of membership fees, with bonus targets linked to gym performance. Other employees are given competitive remuneration including a defined contribution pension scheme and the opportunity to share in the company's success through share incentive plans.

The need for reception staff is eliminated due to the use of the electronic entry system and the online membership and class booking system, other staffing needs such as cleaning, security and non-routine machine maintenance are outsourced which means that gym staff (managers and fitness instructors) are free to concentrate on the core activities of the gym.

The Senior Management Team

The company's senior management team bring to the company a wide range of previous experience mainly in the leisure and retail industries. The team is relatively young, highly enthusiastic and engenders a 'can do' culture throughout the organisation.

The details of the company's executive directors are given below:

Bertram Durand (42) Chief Executive Officer (CEO)

Bertram was appointed as CEO in 2014 and brings to the company extensive experience in the leisure and fitness industry.

Nicola Collette (45) Chief Financial Officer (CFO)

Nicola was appointed as Chief Financial Officer in 2015. She is a professionally qualified accountant. She has been with the company since it started operations in 2005 and was responsible for the company's flotation on the Celtland stock exchange.

Jessica Treewood (38) Marketing Director

Jessica has been with the company since 2014. She holds a BA in Marketing from Celtland University. She previously worked as Marketing Director for a competitor company in the fitness club sector.

Ethan Henson (38) Operations Director

Ethan was appointed Operations Director in 2016. He has responsibility for the running of the gyms and the HR function. He was previously a fitness trainer and has worked his way up through the ranks of the company to become Operations Director.

Gerard Fischer (46) Property Director

Gerard joined the company in 2011 as Property Director. He is responsible for the company's portfolio of properties. He is a qualified civil engineer and has vast experience in property management mainly gained in the hotel industry.

Gemma Schneider (36) IT Director

Gemma joined the company in 2010 as an IT technician and was appointed IT Director in 2017. She holds a MSc in Information Technology. She is keen to further develop GymFit's IT systems with the assistance of her team of innovative and highly qualified staff.

ORGANISATION CHARTS

Executive and non-executive directors

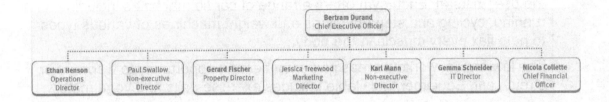

Finance Department

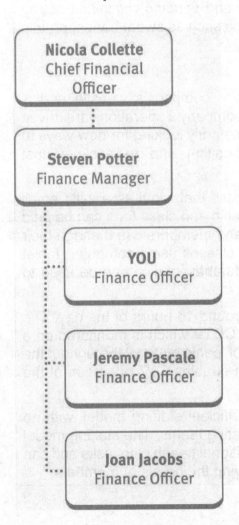

Company Operations

The Gyms

Each gym has more than 150 items of high specification equipment and free weights for members to use. The fitness equipment is eco-friendly with around 70% of the machines using no electricity and are powered by the user instead. Each gym offers a range of cardio machines including running, cycling and step machines and weight machines of various types to help flex every muscle in the body.

The low-impact workout areas give members an opportunity to warm-up or stretch out. Equipment available includes exercise balls and yoga mats.

Each gym contains studios for use by the fitness instructors when leading fitness classes including yoga, Pilates and Dancefit. There are also showers and changing facilities available and vending machines selling bottled drinks and other fitness related items such as sweat bands, protein powder and health bars.

Information Technology (IT)

The IT department runs and manages the company's website and is responsible for website development. The company's operations are driven by technology and the IT department is constantly looking for new ways to utilise IT to improve the member proposition and to achieve cost efficiencies.

GymFit offers a simple online joining process that requires a valid email address and other personal data. Membership and class fees can be paid by credit card, debit card and direct debit and members can manage their accounts, view class timetables and book classes using computer, tablet or mobile. GymFit maintains a customer database which can be used to communicate with members.

Gyms are open 24/7 but only staffed for around 16 hours of the day. The gyms have automated access control and CCTV which is monitored on a 24-hour basis and is enhanced by the use of 'panic buttons' throughout the gym. It is the use of this technology which enables 24/7 operation of the gyms whilst keeping costs low.

The use of technology also results in an efficient staffing model, with no need for dedicated in-gym sales and marketing teams. The staffing model means managers are freed from many traditional health club tasks and can focus on running successful gyms and serving the needs of members.

The extensive use of information technology brings other considerations in terms of system failure, data security and privacy. GymFit's membership system, data processing, account payments, gym access, customer safety and customer marketing, are all dependent on the IT systems. The systems hold a significant amount of confidential customer data including email address, home address and bank details. A breach of data security would constitute a significant risk to the company's reputation and brand.

Marketing

The marketing team's main activities are market research; the promotion and advertising of new and existing gyms; raising brand awareness and advising on pricing strategies. The Marketing team works closely with the IT and Properties department. Marketing efforts are directed at both existing members, to try to ensure member retention, and the recruitment of new members.

The marketing team uses the website to provide members with details of classes being operated each week and any other news or member offers. The customer database is also used to communicate electronically with members using email and SMS.

Regular marketing campaigns ensure that the awareness of the brand is high. A recent campaign featuring a leading Olympic athlete, Johnny Wren, resulted in a 2% increase in member numbers.

Finance

The financial information system produces monthly management accounts and both half-yearly and annual statutory accounts. It also generates daily and weekly sales revenue and membership number information for management to monitor actual results against budgets.

The Finance team also carries out ad-hoc projects including investment appraisal and investigations, along with ongoing decision support. Some areas, including all internal audit work, are delivered by external experts.

Budgets are produced annually using incremental budgeting for sales and cost items. All budgets are broken down into monthly periods, with the exception of the sales budget which is broken down into weekly periods.

Properties

The company has significant experience of developing and managing properties and has been able to use that expertise and its close relationships with suppliers to reduce its fit-out and property management costs.

Growth of the company is dependent on being able to find suitable properties for the new gyms. The company has plans to develop between 15 and 20 properties per year. The majority of properties are leased, for periods of up to 15 years, whilst a small number are owned by the company.

Properties need to be large enough to accommodate the fitness equipment and offer studio space for exercise classes. The ideal property is between 1,000 and 2,000 square metres, over a maximum of two floors. Properties need to be either located within a dense population catchment area to ensure sufficient potential local members or in highly visible locations with easy car parking facilities or access to major transport hubs.

Company Strategy

The company's long-term objective is to deliver long-term profitable growth through improvements in operating efficiency, offering a strong member proposition and by focusing on its people.

It plans to achieve growth through the selective acquisition of existing gym groups, and the lease and fit-out of new properties. The company has a rigorous approach to site selection, with flexible fit-out arrangements allowing the use of a wide variety of building types. It aims to reduce gym fit-out costs through the use of a competitive tender process, negotiating improved terms with suppliers and value engineering the fit-out specification to avoid unnecessary cost.

It plans to achieve improvement to operating efficiency through economies of scale, use of data and technology and also by managing its cost base. The outsourcing of support functions will also enable cost reduction and allow the company to focus on core operations.

In order to continually improve the member proposition, the company will pursue innovative low cost ways to differentiate itself from its competitors. Improvement of member satisfaction, reflected in strong member satisfaction ratings, is a key aim which is dependent on having knowledgeable, well-trained staff. The company strongly believes that attracting, motivating and training people of the highest calibre is key to the company's continued success.

3 The Health and Fitness Industry in Celtland

Celtland health and fitness gym sector is a rapidly growing sector of the health and fitness industry. It has estimated sales revenue of C$7 billion in 2018, an increase of 6.3% on 2017. There are now over 9.7 million people in Celtland who are members of a gym.

This sector experienced modest growth until 2011 thereafter the growth in the market accelerated rapidly, mainly driven by the low-cost segment. Prior to 2011 the market comprised of two main segments: public gyms funded by local government and private gyms funded and operated by commercial enterprises. The rapid increase in low-cost gyms since 2011 has fragmented the market by creating a third segment, low-cost (or budget) gyms, representing 12% of total private gym numbers in 2018.

Gyms are differentiated by a number of factors, including price and contract terms, quality, scope of services and facilities, as well as whether they are part of a larger network.

These can be broadly grouped into:

- Low-cost (or budget) gyms: these are private gyms and differentiate themselves by offering access to gym facilities for a lower price, normally below (depending on the location sometimes well below) C$20 per month. To contain costs, these gyms generally do not offer access to 'wet facilities' (e.g., saunas, steam room, pools), operate large venues (above 1,000 square metres) and can generally be joined online. Also, they will normally transparently advertise their prices online and offer monthly rolling contracts as an option.

- Mid-range and premium gyms: these are also private gyms but are more (or much more) expensive than low-cost gyms. They may, however, offer access to better facilities (e.g. wet facilities or a higher quality environment). These gyms can vary considerably in size, from very small facilities to very large ones. Some gyms will offer monthly rolling contracts and advertise their prices transparently online, others only offer longer-term contracts (e.g. minimum six months or one year) and sometimes require customers to contact the gym to obtain a quote.

- Public gyms: are owned and/or operated by, or on behalf of, local government. The quality of the facilities offered by public gyms can vary considerably. In many instances, public gyms also offer access to wet facilities, including a pool. Their pricing policy also varies considerably. Some business models in the operation of public gyms are similar to those in the categories above.

Recent government initiatives in Celtland, such as the 'GetupGo' campaign, have increased consumers awareness of the negative impact of an inactive lifestyle. The Society of Medical Practitioners have made physical activity one of its top priorities hailing physical activity as the best cure for lifestyle related diseases.

Societal trends have also brought active lifestyles more prominence through the use of Facebook, Instagram and Twitter. These trends have mainly influenced the younger generations who are consequently more health conscious than their predecessors.

Membership profile and customer demand

There are a number of determinants of gym membership with the most important being age; income and educational level.

Previous research studies have shown that the highest percentage of gym members are in the 18-35 age group however the fastest growing sector is the 36-55 age group. Income is a major determinant with households earning $75,000 or more per annum being more likely to have gym membership. However, within the high earners segment ($75,000 and above) educational level was a significant factor with around 25% of those with degree level education having gym membership compared to less than 12% of those who did not go to University or College.

The overall penetration rate in Celtland is 14.3% but demand will be influenced by the members' proximity to the gym with most gym members being within 12 minutes driving time of the gym. Proximity to good road or rail network will be a contributing factor. The extent of competition in the specific areas will also be an important factor in estimating potential demand.

Competitive Situation

Within the low-cost gym sector in Celtland there are four major players including GymFit. GymFit is the second largest operator in the sector in terms of number of gyms. The largest operator Gym4All has grown mainly through the acquisition of other smaller gym groups. A number of smaller gym groups, typically operating between ten and thirty gyms, still remain.

The rising star in the Celtland market is Fit4Life which has ruthlessly marketed itself as a lifelong alternative to the other low-cost gyms. Fit4Life offers members a lifelong membership fee which will not increase provided the customer remains a member. Its rapid growth has also been driven by its use of specialised fitness apps which have been developed using data analytics. These apps provide members with tailored personal training advice and programmes which they can access at home.

Future Outlook

Growth in the Celtland health and fitness gym market is strong and steady and is expected to continue for the next few years driven by technology changes and government initiatives to improve health and fitness.

The Celtland health and fitness gym market is relatively immature compared to similar markets in Europe. Norway, Sweden and the Netherlands all have mature markets with penetration rates of 19.4%, 16.7% and 16.4% respectively. These penetration rates indicate that there is potential for a strong increase in overall member numbers compared to Celtland's current penetration rate of 14.3%.

Whilst membership numbers are growing, operators still face the challenge of member retention. Technology can minimise cancellations by making the gym experience more enjoyable and rewarding, but operators must work to provide a service that members can't get from exercising alone or by going elsewhere.

The increasing presence of virtual reality (VR), immersive experiences and video-on-demand (VOD) is one way health and fitness clubs can achieve member retention. These technologies allow gym operators to provide content in multiple locations at once, while freeing up instructors. From a member perspective, VOD fitness can be accessed anywhere and at any time thus eliminating the need to be at a gym at a certain time, or at all. Apps and online channels also offer operators a way to help member's access VOD fitness classes at home or away.

4   Extract from GymFit's 2018 Consolidated Financial Statements

Statement of Profit or Loss for the year ended 31 December	2018 C$000	2017 C$000
Revenue	73,102	58,831
Operating expenses		
Gym operating costs	(20,389)	(16,384)
Lease costs	(13,840)	(10,800)
Staff costs	(10,561)	(7,955)
Head office costs	(7,280)	(5,840)
Depreciation	(11,524)	(10,154)
Amortisation	(940)	(1,154)
Total operating expenses	(64,533)	(52,287)
Operating profit	8,569	6,544
Finance Income	12	12
Finance costs	(612)	(633)
Profit before tax	7,969	5,923)
Taxation	(1,616)	(990)
Profit / (loss) for the year	6,353	4,933

Statement of Pro Financial Position as at 31 December	2018 C$000	2017 C$000
Non-current assets		
Intangible assets	49,653	48,974
Tangible assets	107,150	69,352
Investment	200	200
	157,003	118,526
Current assets		
Inventories	158	127
Trade receivables	7,229	4,651
Cash and cash equivalents	366	3,858
Total Assets	7,753	8,636
	164,756	127,162
Equity and Liabilities		
Share capital	48	48
Share premium	79,027	79,027
Retained earnings	17,632	12,357
Total equity	96,707	91,432
Non-current liabilities		
Borrowings	32,071	8,325
	32,071	8,325
Current liabilities		
Trade payables	35,320	27,298
Bank loans and overdraft	0	0
Current tax liabilities	658	107
	35,978	27,405
Total Equity and Liabilities	164,756	127,162

Statement of Cash Flows or the year ended 31 December	2018 C$000	2017 C$000
Cash flows from operating activities		
Profit / (loss) before tax	7,969	5,923
Depreciation	11,523	10,154
Amortisation	940	1,154
Net finance costs	600	621
(Increase) / decrease in inventory	(31)	(30)
(Increase) / decrease in trade and other receivables	(2,578)	(128)
Increase / (decrease) in trade and other payables	8,022	6,862
Cash generated from operations	26,445	24,556
Interest paid	(612)	(633)
Tax paid	(1,065)	(882)
Net cash generated from operating activities	24,768	23,041
Cash flows from investing activities		
Purchase of tangible assets	(49,321)	(21,374)
Purchase of intangibles	(1,619)	(818)
Interest received	12	12
Net cash used in investing activities	(50,928)	(22,180)
Cash flows from financing activities		
Increase / (repayment) of long-term borrowings	23,746	966
Dividend paid	(1,078)	(257)
Net cash from/ (used in) financing activities	22,668	709
Net increase / (decrease) in cash and cash equivalents	(3,492)	1,570
Cash and cash equivalents at beginning of the year	3,858	2,288
Cash and cash equivalents at the end of the year	366	3,858

5   Budget information 2019

Membership Fee Budget 2019

		City	Town	Total
Number of gyms		30	86	116
Average number of members per gym	**Full-fee**	3,660	3,107	3,250
	Student	1,396	1,199	1,250
	Total	5,056	4,306	4,500
Average membership fee per month (C$)	**Full-fee**	21.96	12.14	15.00
	Student	17.59	9.73	12.00
Total membership fees per year (C$000)	**Full-fee**	28,934	38,926	67,860
	Student	8,840	12,040	20,880
	Total	37,774	50,966	88,740

Sales Budget 2019

Number of gyms		116	
Average number of members per gym		4,500	
Total sales revenue (C$000)		92,394	
	Per member C$	**Number of members per gym**	**Total C$000**
Average membership fees	170.00	4,500	88,740
Classes	5.28	4,500	2,756
Vending machine income	1.45	4,500	757
Day passes			141
Total sales revenue			92,394

Operating Profit Budget 2019

	Total		Per gym	
	$000	$000	$000	$000
		92,394		796
Sales revenue				
Operating expenses	(23,920)		(206)	
Gym operating costs	(16,991)		(146)	
Lease costs	(11,822)		(102)	
Staff costs	(8,221)		(71)	
Depreciation	(14,616)		(126)	
Amortisation	(23,920)		(9)	
	(1,040)	(76,610)		(660)
Operating profit		15,784		136

GymFit Key Statistics

	Budget 2019	Actual 2018	Actual 2017	Actual 2016
Total number of gyms	116	102	71	59
New gym openings	14	31	12	15
*Number of mature gyms	71	59	44	32
Total number of members	548,100	485,600	358,400	300,800
Average number of members	522,000	422,586	344,066	283,908
Average number of members per gym	4,500	4,143	4,846	4,846
Total sales revenue (C$000)	92,394	73,101	58,831	47,983
Sales revenue per member per year	$177	$173	$171	$169
Total number of operational employees	225	198	138	114

*Mature gyms are those gyms which have been operating for more than 2 years.

6　The Tax Regime in Celtland

Corporate Profits:

- The corporate tax rate applicable to taxable profits is 20%.
- The sales tax rate is 20%.
- Unless otherwise stated below, accounting rules on recognition and measurement are followed for tax purposes.
- The following expenses are not allowable for tax purposes:
  - accounting depreciation; o amortisation;
  - entertaining expenditure;
  - donations to political parties; and
  - Taxes paid to other public bodies.
- Tax depreciation allowances are available on items of plant and machinery (including vehicles used for business purposes) at a rate of 25% per year on a reducing balance basis.
- Tax losses can be carried forward to offset against future taxable profits from the same business.

Fitness Monthly

16 January 2019   No. 78   C$4.70

Is data analytics the future for the fitness industry?

Georgio Duccatti – **Business Correspondent**

We live in a world driven by technology. The fitness industry is no exception, as the opportunity to use technology and data promises a step change in the gym experience. We are beginning to see collaborations between brands that have created connectivity between a wide variety of fitness equipment, devices, wearable technology and healthcare apps.

These collaborations offer us a much broader view of fitness, health and preferences. The resulting data has the power to fundamentally change our behaviour. It is no surprise then that the market for connected gym equipment is growing at an incredible rate, estimated at over 40% per year.

Imagine tracking changes in important body statistics, working through an automated training programme that has been designed based on your likes, dislikes, goals and progress.

The gym benefits too. By understanding your profile and preferences, the gym can align their offer, for example adapting classes and facilities. This increases member loyalty and reduces churn.

The amount of data that could be created is huge, along with the possibilities. It is still relatively early days but the size of the opportunity is clear.

Fitness Monthly

6 February 2019   No. 78   C$4.70

The battle to beat inactivity – are we winning?

Georgio Duccatti – **Business Correspondent**

According to a recent report by the Celtland Heart Disease Research Foundation the answer is a resounding 'No'.

The report suggests that more than 20 million people in Celtand are physically inactive and the charity warns that inactivity increases the risk of heart disease.

The Celtland government recently announced its GetupGo initiative to try to encourage both adults and children to exercise on a regular basis.

GetupGo heralds a new approach which shifts the balance of investment, for the first time, to focus more on encouraging inactive and under-represented groups to become more active. It is believed that this is where the greatest individual, community and economic gains can be made.

The government is encouraging community group, health care providers, employers and local authorities to take action to support the initiative.

Private sector companies in the health and fitness sector are also being encouraged to target new members from these under-represented groups.

So, if you're not already a member of a gym then maybe it's time to 'get up and go' down to your local gym. You might be pleasantly surprised at the offers available!!

2019 Prototype exam – analysing the pre-seen

Chapter learning objectives

- to understand various techniques and models that can help familiarisation with the pre-seen.

1 The importance of familiarisation

The pre-seen material is released approximately seven weeks before you sit the exam and one of your first tasks will be to analyse the context within which the case is set. Although your responses in the exam will be driven by the unseen material, you will only be able to fully assess the impact of each event on the organisation if you have a sufficient depth of knowledge and awareness of both the organisation and the industry in which it operates.

The purpose of the pre-seen material is to allow you to gain that knowledge and awareness. Remember, you will be acting in the position of a management accountant who works for the organisation in a finance officer role. It will therefore be expected that you will have the same level of familiarisation as someone fulfilling that role.

It is extremely important that you study the pre-seen material thoroughly before you go into the examination. There are two main reasons for this:

- It will save time in the examination itself if you are already familiar with the pre-seen material (especially in relation to how any costing information is presented).

- It enables you to develop a view of the situation facing the organisation in the case study.

You will not be able to respond to the examination tasks from the pre-seen material alone; the unseen material given to you in the examination will present significant new information that may alter the situation substantially. Even so, a major step towards success in the examination is a careful study, exploration and understanding of the pre-seen material.

Each set of pre-seen material is different but as a general rule, you can expect the following:

- Industry background

- History of the business

- Key personnel

- Current business/industry issues

- Management accounting information, such as costing schedules

- Financial Statements

- Tax regime

Each of these areas will need reviewing in detail.

You should question what each piece of information tells you, and why the examiner may have given it to you.

2 Exhibit by exhibit analysis

The purpose of this initial stage is to lay a foundation for further analysis. It's more about asking questions than finding solutions. Before you do anything else, you should read the pre-seen material from beginning to end without making any notes, simply to familiarise yourself with the scenario.

Read the material again, as many times as you think necessary, without making notes. You can do this over a period of several days, if you wish.

When you think you are reasonably familiar with the situation described by the material, you should start to make notes. By making notes, you will become more familiar with the detail of the scenario.

- Try to make notes on each paragraph (or each group of short paragraphs) in the pre-seen material.

- Ask yourself "why might the examiner have told me this?"

- Try to make your questions as broad as possible; consider as many different stakeholders as possible and try to put yourself in different positions (say the CEO, a customer, an employee, etc.) to consider the information from different perspectives.

Illustration 1 – GymFit: Introductory overview

Given below is an example of some questions you could ask yourself relating to the second exhibit of the "question tutorial" exam pre-seen information.

Question	Potential response
What does GymFit do?	Low cost, no frills, no contract approach to running a gym.
Is GymFit a major player?	2nd largest operator of low cost gyms in Celtland.
What is GymFit's pricing strategy?	Gym managers can set their own fees. If clients want additional lessons with fitness instructors, say, then they negotiate these with the instructor.
How important is IT to GymFit?	Critical – clients join/pay on the website, clients can view schedules on mobile devices, electronic entry to gyms, etc all these allow the company to employ fewer staff.
What are the key elements of the company's strategy to deliver growth?	(1) Improvements in operating efficiency, (2) Offering a strong member proposition and by, (3) Focusing on its people.

3   Note taking

When you're making notes, try to be as creative as possible. Psychologists tell us that using conventional linear notes on their own use only a small part of our mental capacity. They are hard to remember and prevent us from drawing connections between topics. This is because they seek to classify things under hierarchical headings.

Here are some techniques that candidates find useful. See which ones work for you as you practise on the "question tutorial" case in this text.

Spider diagrams

Spider diagrams (or clustering diagrams) are a quick graphic way of summarising connections between subjects. You cannot put much detail into a spider diagram, just a few key words. However, it does help you to 'visualise' the information in the case material. You must expect to update your spider diagram as you go along and to redraft it when it starts to get too messy. It is all part of the learning process.

Timelines

Timelines are valuable to make sense of the sequence of events in the pre-seen and to understand where the company in the case study presently stands. The case study exam takes place in real time, so you need to be clear how long is likely to elapse between the data in the pre-seen and the actual exam. This is the time period during which the issues facing the company can be incorporated into the unseen material.

Colours

Colours help you remember things you may want to draw upon in the exam room. You could write down all your financial calculations and observations in green whilst having red for organisational and blue for strategic. Some candidates use different colour highlighter pens to emphasise different aspects of the pre-seen material perhaps using the same colour coding suggestion.

Additionally, sometimes making notes in different colours helps you to remember key facts and some of the preparation that you have done using the pre-seen material.

Use whatever colours work for you – but it does help to make notes on both the pre-seen material and the research you do. DO NOT just read the material – you must take notes (in whatever format) and if colours help you to understand and link your research together then use colours.

4 Technical analysis

Now you're reasonably familiar with the material it's time to carry out some technical analysis to help you identify and understand the issues facing the company.

A good starting point is to revise any 'technical' topics that might be relevant. The pre-seen material might make a reference to a particular 'technical' issue, such as possible constraints in production / operation, costing or pricing issues, budget approach, performance issues, financial reporting issues and so on. Anticipate exam tasks by asking yourself how you would apply these models in the context of the live case.

If you lack confidence on any topic that might be relevant, go back to your previous study materials and revise it if necessary.

Exercise 1 – GymFit: P1 topic analysis

Typical P1 topic areas (that could be applied to any case) include the following.

1   Discuss which costs are fixed and which variable.

2   Discuss how useful overhead absorption is to GymFit in terms of (a) splitting costs between gyms and (b) splitting costs within gyms.

3   How useful do you think ABC would be to GymFit?

4   Discuss whether an incremental or ZBB approach would be most suitable for GymFit.

5   Suggest four variances that would be of most use to GymFiT. Justify your choices.

5 Financial analysis

You will almost certainly be given some figures in the pre-seen material. These might relate to the company's profits or losses, or product profitability. There might be statements of profit or loss and statements of financial position for previous years, future business plans, cash flow statements, capital expenditure plans, and so on.

A key part of your initial analysis will be to perform some simple financial analysis, such as financial ratio calculations or a cash flow analysis. These might give you a picture of changes in profitability, liquidity, working capital management or cash flows over time, and will help ensure you have a rounded picture of the organisation's current position.

If a cash flow statement is not provided, it may be worth preparing a summary of cash flows. You may have to make some assumptions if the detailed information isn't provided but even with these, there is great value in appreciating where the money has come from, and where it is being spent.

Profitability ratios

You might find useful information from an analysis of profit/sales ratios, for:

- the company as a whole

- each division, or

- each product or service.

Profit margins can be measured as a net profit percentage and as a gross profit percentage. You can then look at trends in the ratios over time, or consider whether the margins are good or disappointing.

Analysing the ratio of certain expenses to sales might also be useful, such as the ratio of administration costs to sales, sales and marketing costs to sales or R&D costs to sales. Have there been any noticeable changes in these ratios over time and, if so, is it clear why the changes have happened?

Working capital ratios

Working capital ratios can be calculated to assess the efficiency of working capital management (= management of inventory, trade receivables and trade payables). They can also be useful for assessing liquidity, because excessive investment in working capital ties up cash and slows the receipt of cash.

The main working capital ratios are:

- "inventory days" or the average inventory holding period: a long period might indicate poor inventory management

- "receivable days" or the average time that customers take to pay: a long period could indicate issues with the collection of cash, although would need to consider this in light of the entity's credit terms and industry averages

- "payable days" or the average time to pay suppliers: a long period could indicate cash flow difficulties for the entity, although would need to consider in light of credit terms.

You should be familiar with these ratios and how to calculate the length of the cash cycle or operating cycle.

Cash flow analysis or funding analysis

If the main objective of a company is to maximise the wealth of its shareholders, the most important financial issues will be profitability and returns to shareholders. However, other significant issues in financial strategy are often:

- cash flows and liquidity, and

- funding

A possible cash flow problem occurs whenever the cash flows from operations do not appear to be sufficient to cover all the non-operational cash payments that the company has to make, such as spending on capital expenditure items.

An analysis of future funding can be carried out by looking at the history of changes in the statement of financial position.

Exercise 2 – GymFit: Ratio Analysis

Complete the following table and answer the questions below.

Ratio	2019 (budget)	2018	2019
Growth in revenue			
Growth in gym operating costs			
Growth in lease costs			
Growth in staff costs			
Growth in head office costs			
Growth in depreciation			
Growth in operating profit			
Operating margin			
Inventory days			
Receivables days			
Payables days			
Length of operating cycle			

Questions

1   Did GymFit perform well in 2018?

2   Why had revenue increased in 2018?

3   Comment on the increase in costs between 2017 and 18.

4   Had the working capital position worsened or improved? Explain.

5   Comment on GymFit's financial gearing.

6   Comment on GymFit's cash flow.

7   Discuss whether the 2019 budget is realistic.

6   Industry analysis and research

The relevance of industry research

There is little credit in the exam for real world comments (especially since the 2019 syllabus update) and, at the operational level, the idea of the pre-seen is that you will have everything you need to know. If you know this inside out and have the technical knowledge at your fingertips in the exam to apply to the task, then you are giving yourself the best chance of passing.

Furthermore, a review of examiner's comments reveals that it is much more important to ensure you have revised the technical content from P1 and F1, than it is to do extensive background research.

Given the above, you could question whether any industry research is worthwhile. The purpose of doing at least some research is as follows:

- To help you develop a better understanding of the problems (and opportunities) facing companies in this industry and so prioritise issues.

- To give you greater reassurance that you understand the industry and haven't missed anything important in the pre-seen

- By considering the strategies followed by real world companies and whether they could be adopted by the company in the pre-seen will help you analyse possible exam scenarios.

- This should mean that you will be able to understand, analyse and answer exam tasks more quickly and confidently.

- Hopefully, it will also stop you from making unrealistic comments in your answer on the day of the exam.

Ultimately it is a matter of achieving a balance between revising technical aspects and performing additional research that will help you put yourself in the position of the finance officer.

How to conduct industry research

As stated above, at operational level you will not be expected to undertake vast amounts of your own research into the industry. Having said that, such research will help you to more fully understand some of the issues affecting the organisation and to put yourself in the shoes of the person that you will need to be in the exam room. Therefore this section will give you some ideas and tools to help with this research.

Your research could incorporate any of the following sources of information:

- *Personal networks / experience*

  It may be that you have been a customer in the industry described. For the sample paper, many students would have had experience of being a gym member and so would appreciate some of the issues involved.

- *Using the Internet*

  This is the most convenient and commonly used method of researching the industry, but as noted above, try to target the information you're looking for in order to avoid wasting time. Generally, you will be looking for the following sorts of information:

  - Websites of firms similar to the one(s) in the pre-seen material. This can help you learn about the sorts of products and competitive strategies they follow.

  - Articles on the industry in journals and newspapers. These will keep you up to date on developments.

Illustration 2 – GymFit: Real world websites

Relevant websites for the gym industry include the following:

Industry in general:

https://www.theguardian.com/lifeandstyle/shortcuts/2017/may/08/the-budget-gym-boom-how-low-cost-clubs-are-driving-up-membership - looks at the rise of low cost gyms

https://www.moneysavingexpert.com/deals/cheap-gym-membership - gives idea of promotional activities used by gyms

Budget gym operators:

https://www.puregym.com/

http://www.fitness4less.co.uk/

7 Ethical analysis

Before the exam, you should take some time to remind yourself of CIMA's Guidelines on ethical conduct. Although these are useful, you must remember that the ethical issues in the exam are not necessarily ethical issues facing the management accountant, but more issues facing the business as a whole.

Ethical issues could this relate to any of the following areas:

- corporate social responsibility;
- personal ethical behaviour of individuals in the case;
- business ethics.

Illustration 3 – GymFit: Real world ethical issues

Online research into gyms quickly reveals ethical (and legal) issues related to onerous membership contracts. For example,

http://www.independent.co.uk/news/business/news/gym-group-may-have-legal-questions-to-answer-over-contracts-says-gig-economy-law-firm-that-a8036346.html

8 Position audit

Once you've analysed all of the above you're ready to carry out a position audit.

CIMA defines a position audit as:

Part of the planning process which examines the current state of the entity in respect of:

- resources of tangible and intangible assets and finance,
- products brands and markets,
- operating systems such as production and distribution,

- internal organisation,
- current results,
- returns to stockholders.

What you should be attempting to do is stand back so you can appreciate the bigger picture of the organisation. You can do this by considering four main headings – Strengths, Weaknesses, Opportunities and Threats. This is usually referred to as a SWOT analysis.

In general terms, threats and opportunities (and even weaknesses) can help you see where the scenario for the business might go and hence what the scenarios in the cases might be and therefore likely tasks.

More specifically, within your SWOT analysis you should look for:

- Threats homing in upon weaknesses – the potential for failure.
- Threats linked to strengths – should be able to defend against it but remember competencies slip.
- Opportunities linked to a strength – areas they should be able to exploit.
- Opportunities linked to weaknesses – areas where they could exploit in the future if they can change.

Exercise 3 – GymFit: SWOT analysis
Perform a SWOT analysis for GymFit.

9 Main issues and précis

In addition to preparing a SWOT analysis, it is useful to prepare a two-three page summary of your analysis. Try not to simply repeat information from the pre-seen but add value by including your thoughts on the analysis you've performed.

Once you've prepared your summary you are finally able to consider the key issues facing the organisation. Your conclusion on the main issues arising from the pre-seen will direct your focus and aid your understanding of issues in the exam.

Once you've got a list of the main issues, give yourself more time to think. Spend some time thinking about the case study, as much as you can. You don't have to be sitting at a desk or table to do this. You can think about the case study when you travel to work or in any spare time that you have for thinking.

- When new ideas come to you, jot them down.
- If you think of a new approach to financial analysis, carry out any calculations you think might be useful.

Remember, all of the above preparatory work enables you to feel as if you really are a management accountant working for this organisation. Without the prep, you're unlikely to be convincing in this role.

Illustration 4 – GymFit: Summary

The pre-seen information concerns a company called GymFit that offers low-cost gym membership in the country of Celtland.

Business model

GymFit offers low-cost, no-frills gym membership with no contracts. Despite having low fees, the company provides high quality gym equipment. The 'no-frills' aspect is that they do not provide swimming pools, saunas, restaurants or bars.

Key to low fees is keeping costs low (e.g. through competitive tendering when fitting out new gyms), outsourcing non-core aspects such as security and the use of technology to reduce staffing needs. Each gym typically has two employees – a manager and an assistant manager. A key aspect of staffing is the use of freelance fitness instructors on zero-hour contracts

Growth has involved a mixture of organic growth and acquisition.

This strategy has been successful to date and the company is now the second largest low-cost gym in Celtland with 102 gyms and turnover in excess of C£73 million.

Competition

There are four major players in the low-cost sector in Celtland. The largest, Gym4All has grown primarily by acquisitions but the main threat comes from Fit4Life, who offers lifelong membership and has developed specialist fitness apps to enhance the customer experience.

Given the above, customer retention is now seen as a critical success factor in the industry.

Financial performance

Revenue grew by 24% from 2016 to 2017, resulting in an increase of 31% in operating profit. This also increased operating margins from 11.1% to 11.7%.

The overall level of investment in non-current assets grew substantially (55%), reflecting aggressive growth plans by the Board.

In terms of working capital and liquidity, cash fell by C$3.5 million and borrowing increased by C$24, reflecting the fact that considerable finance was needed to fund expansion and that, even with the additional debt, the company had a net cash outflow of C$3.5m. It is questionable how future growth will be financed.

Inventory days and receivables increased significantly, indicating that the company may be struggling to cope with the high growth experienced.

Future prospects

The market is expected to continue to grow, fuelled by low penetration rates compared to other European countries, government initiatives such as 'GetupGo' and technological developments.

It is vital that GymFit capitalises on these developments and does not get left behind.

Stated strategy

GymFit wants to continue to grow through a mixture of new gyms and acquisition.

In addition it wants to improve operating efficiency through economies of scale, outsourcing and the use of data and technology.

Finally, it wants to improve member satisfaction, linked primarily to having knowledgeable, well-trained staff.

Budgeting

Budgets are prepared on an annual basis GymFit adopts a participative approach to price setting, which should give better ownership of budgets but may result in budgetary 'slack' and 'padding', especially as gym managers have a bonus system linked to gym performance.

Budgeted sales for 2018 give an increase in revenue of 26% over 2017, which is higher growth than achieved last year, despite opening fewer new gyms. Overall the budget looks overly optimistic.

10 Summary

You should now understand what you need to do in order to familiarise yourself with the pre-seen sufficiently.

Test your understanding answers

Exercise 1 – GymFit: P1 topic analysis

1   Discuss which costs are fixed and which variable.

Costs that vary with the number of customers/members are likely to be

- An element of energy costs – e.g. heating water for showers
- An element of water costs if charged for usage
- An element of cleaning costs, although this may be totally fixed within the cleaning contract
- An element of the cost of providing free fitness classes
- An element of the maintenance cost of equipment.

Costs that vary with the number of gyms

- Most gym operating costs such as lighting, the fixed element of water bills, aspects of cleaning costs, etc
- Gym lease costs
- Gym staff costs

All other costs, such as head office rent, will be fixed.

2   Discuss how useful overhead absorption is to GymFit in terms of (a) splitting costs between gyms and (b) splitting costs within gyms.

It may be that head office costs are split between gyms (p18) for performance evaluation purposes but it is unclear whether they actually do this and, if so, how. In any case, unless such costs are directly attributable to the gym's existence, then they should not be included when assessing the gym. Similarly, unless the costs are in some way controllable by the gym manager, then they should not be included for their performance appraisal. Either way, it is unlikely that splitting costs between gyms is very useful.

There is also no indication that they do any overhead absorption within gyms and, again, it is probably of little use to them:

- Inventory valuation – they are a service provider rather than a manufacturer, so don't have to determine the full cost (including overheads) of goods for inventory purposes

- Pricing – they only have one basic revenue stream (membership) so there is no need to split costs between different sources within gyms in order to help price them – e.g. fees for trainers are paid directly to trainers.

- There is no indication that the gyms are broken down into different cost centres as the no-frills concept means that the usual cost centres of a restaurant, bars, pool, etc, do not exist.

The only exception to the above could be a need to apportion costs to classes in order to determine how much to charge for them, but classes only account for 3% of total revenue (p17).

3   How useful do you think ABC would be to GymFit?

The main benefit of ABC is that it gives a more useful split of costs between products / cost centres. For the reasons given above in the answer to Q2, not very.

4   Discuss whether an incremental or ZBB approach would be most suitable for GymFit.

GymFit currently does incremental budgeting.

Incremental budgeting is generally seen to be appropriate when there is no change in product range – this is true for GymFit.

Incremental budgeting is also useful where there is no change in customers or target markets. This is less true as 31 new gyms were opened in 2018 with plans for an additional 14 in 2019 (p19). Every time there is a new gym, then it could be argued that a ZBB would be more appropriate.

Furthermore, GymFit has grown by acquisition. Again ZBB will be more useful here as GymFit will want to make changes to gyms acquired and may not be able to trust previous budgets.

5   Identify four variances of use for GymFit.

Sales mix variances – GymFiT charges lower fees to students (p17) so management would want to see how the mix of customers varies from budget.

Lease cost expenditure variances – A key element of growth is finding suitable new premises, many of which are leased. Lease costs are the second largest cost category after operating costs (p18) so it is vital that management can see if leases on new gyms are more expensive than expected.

Cost expenditure variances for out-sourced operations such as cleaning and security – The company strategy (p11) includes a need to reduce costs. These cost variances could indicate the extent to which outsourcing is delivering such reductions.

Gym operating cost expenditure and efficiency variances – Operating costs are the largest category of cost (p14) and , as stated above, the company is looking to improve efficiency

Exercise 2 – GymFit: Ratio Analysis

Complete the following table and answer the questions below.

Ratio	2019 (budget)	2018	2019
Growth in revenue	26.4%	24.2%	
Growth in gym operating costs	17.3%	24.4%	
Growth in lease costs	22.8%	28.1%	
Growth in staff costs	11.9%	32.8%	
Growth in head office costs	12.9%	24.6%	
Growth in depreciation	26.8%	13.5%	
Growth in operating profit	84.2%	30.9%	
Operating margin	17.1%	11.7%	11.1%
Inventory days		3	3
Receivables days		36	29
Payables days		311	302
Length of operating cycle		–	–

Notes:

1   Inventory days have been calculated using gym operating costs. Ideally we would have the purchases figure for vending machine items. Bottled water, etc, so the figure calculated will be too low

2   Payables days have been calculated using gym operating costs + lease costs + head office costs. However, the figures that result seem extremely high, suggesting that 'trade creditors' includes more than what is owed to external cleaning, maintenance and security suppliers and utilities providers. It probably includes amounts owed for new gym equipment, for example.

3   Given the above, the resulting operating cycle figures are not likely to be very meaningful.

Questions

1   Did GymFit perform well in 2018?

Positives

- Overall profit for the year up 29% from C$4.9m to C$6.4m

- Revenue up 24%

- Operating profit up 31%

- Operating margins up from 11.1% to 11.7%

- Significant investment in new gyms and equipment

Negatives

- Many costs went up by more than revenue
- Significant drop in cash balances
- Significant increase in long term borrowing
- Significant increase in both receivables and payables

2   Why had turnover increased in 2018?

- Total number of gyms went up 44% from 71 to 102
- Average number of members went up 23% from 344k to 423k
- Average revenue per member went up 1% from $171 to $173
- This will be the result of a strong member proposition, a commitment to opening new gyms and successful advertising
- Note – the average membership per gym fell from 4,846 to 4,14

3   Comment on the increase in costs between 2017 and 18.

As discussed above, many costs are likely to be fixed per gym rather than fixed for the business as a whole. Therefore, each time a new gym is opened we should expect these costs to increase (gym operating, lease, staff etc). From 2017 to 2018 the number of gyms increased by 44%, so we would expect a 44% increase in these costs. However, this was not the case:

- Gym operating costs increased 24%
- Lease costs increased 28%
- Staff costs increased 33%

This either indicates that new gyms are becoming less expensive to open and operate, or that GymFit has gained costs efficiencies in existing gyms in line with their stated intent of cost cutting in their strategy.

4   Had the working capital position worsened or improved? Explain.

Worsened

- Cash fallen by C$3.5m
- Receivables increased by C$2.6m
- Receivables days increased from 29 to 36 days

5   Comment on GymFit's financial gearing.

Increased significantly

- Long term borrowings up by C$23.7m
- This means higher gearing risk for shareholders

6 Comment on GymFit's cash flow.

Positives

- Cash generated by operations increased to over C$26.4m

- Able to invest C$49.3m in new tangible assets

- Able to pay C$1m dividend, a significant increase on 2017

Negatives

- Net cash outflow – spent C$3.5m more cash than raised/generated

- Had to increase debt and reduce cash balances to finance growth – is this sustainable?

7 Discuss whether the 2019 budget is realistic.

Aspects that seem realistic / reasonable

- Average sales revenue per member only increasing by 1%

- Only opening 14 new gyms in 2019 compared with 31 in 2018

- 14 new gyms (14%) are planned to be opened in 2019, so would expect many gym related costs to increase by this amount. Gym lease costs are expected to increase by 23% possibly implying that new leases are more expensive. Similarly operating costs are expected to increase by 17%, which, if anything might be seen to overly pessimistic rather than optimistic.

Aspects that seem to be over-optimistic

- 26% growth in revenue compared to 24% in 2018 seems high, especially given that we are only opening 14 new gyms vs 31. The growth must therefore be heavily dependent on retaining existing customers and winning new ones for existing gyms as well as looking for growth by opening gyms. This is seen in the average gym membership increasing from 4,143 to 4,500 but it is unclear how such confidence can be justified, particularly as average gym membership fell from 2017 to 2018.

- As stated above, would expect many gym related costs to increase by 14% but staff costs are expected to increase by 12%. While this could indicate over-optimism, it is more likely to be due to planned reductions in staff costs and/or the fact that some gyms would not have been open for the full year.

- Operating margin increasing from 11.7% to 17.1%

- Operating profit increasing by 84%

Overall, the budget looks optimistic / challenging

Exercise 3 – GymFit: SWOT analysis

Strengths

- Gyms are located with excellent access to public transport links and/or good parking
- Wide range of high-specification, eco-friendly gym equipment (70% use no electricity)
- 24/7 gym operating hours – attractive to members
- No-contract membership with option of pay-as-you-use basis
- Historic growth is forecast to continue
- Simple functional structure which suits the company's size/lack of diversification
- 2nd largest operator of low-cost gyms in Celtland
- One of the pioneers of the low-cost gym model
- Listed on the Celtland stock exchange
- Some free classes, free induction session
- Gyms have showers, changing areas, lockers and vending machines
- Advanced technology
- Members can join, manage their accounts, view class timetables and book classes online
- Simple online joining process
- Efficient staffing model, no need for receptionists (PIN entry system), in-gym sales, etc
- Fitness instructors are trained experts
- Experienced, highly enthusiastic senior management team (e.g. in developing and managing properties)
- Knowledgeable, well-trained staff
- 'Can do' culture throughout the organisation
- Gym managers have bonus targets linked to gym performance
- Competitive remuneration for employees, including pension scheme and opportunity to take part in a share incentive plan
- Recognise the need for continued investment in marketing
- Customer database used to communicate with members
- CCTV, panic buttons in the gyms
- Well-used website e.g. details of weekly classes
- Regular marketing campaigns ensure high brand awareness
- Healthy financials – revenue, profit increased.

Weaknesses

- No wet facilities e.g. saunas/ pools
- No cafes / bars
- Fitness instructors may be dissatisfied with zero hours contracts
- Extensive use of IT leads to associated risks of system failure, data security and privacy. This can impact the company's reputation.
- High levels of receivables
- May be trying to grow too quickly as evidenced by a large fall in cash and increase in debt to finance new gyms

Opportunities

- Develop app-based technology, similar to Fit4Life to provide tailored personal fitness advice
- Use VR and VOD to improve member retention
- Collaboration to create connectivity between fitness equipment, devices, wearable technology and healthcare apps
- Harness data from such collaborations/ connected gym equipment to help understand customers' preferences, adapt classes and facilities etc.
- Work with the Celtland government to encourage under-represented groups to exercise more
- Organic growth in Celtland – increase number of gyms each year
- Merger with/acquisition of budget gym competitors
- Expand outside Celtland
- Further use of a celebrity to promote brand (Sir Chris Hoy is an 'ambassador' for PureGym in the UK)
- Offer corporate membership to businesses
- Open boutique gyms (under a different brand?)
- Ladies only facilities?
- Link with sportswear company to promote product through GymFit website/premises
- Improve operating efficiency through economies of scale, use of data and technology and managing its cost base
- Pursue innovative low cost ways to differentiate from competitors

Threats

- Increased competitive pressure from rivals – especially FiT4Life and Gym4ALL

- Gym membership is discretionary (non-essential) spending, so overall demand may be heavily influenced by the state of the economy.

- Failure of IT systems – membership enrolment, account management, payment processing, gym access and customer communications are all dependant on the successful operation of information systems

- Breach of data security - unauthorised access or loss of information could lead to legal claims, disruption to operations and reputational damage.

- The loss of key staff, both at gym level and managerial level could lead to a lack of experienced and motivated staff which would impact on the customer experience and on other central business functions.

- Failure to provide customers with a high quality, affordable and accessible service would result in a decrease in customer numbers and revenue and would also damage GymFit's reputation.

- Health and safety – serious injury to a member whilst no staff present results in litigation/loss of reputation

- GymFit outsources a number of our non-core business processes, such as security, maintenance and cleaning. Failure to meet the high standards expected of these outsourced operators would impact on the customer experience and potentially their overall safety in the gyms. This could result in a reduction in customer numbers and a loss of revenue.

Note: you could then use the above analysis to envisage possible exam storylines, scenarios and tasks.

For example, taking the threat of competitive rivalry, one scenario could be that some gyms are underperforming, so the Board are considering whether to close them.

An exam style task could then be to discuss how you assess the performance of gyms anyway?

- What KPIs would you focus on and

- What sources of information would you look at?

Alternatively, how would you make the decision whether to close a particular gym?

- Hopefully you recognise that such a decision should be made by reference to relevant costing principles, so any head office recharges should be excluded, for example.

- Obviously the impact on sales is a relevant cash flow but how would you estimate this? Do you think customers would be lost or would some use a nearby gym instead?

This analysis can then prompt you to revise the relevant technical areas if you are unsure of any.

Exam day techniques

Chapter learning objectives

- To develop a carefully planned and thought through strategy to cope with the three hours of exam time

1 Exam day strategy

Once you have studied the pre-seen, learnt the three subject syllabi thoroughly and practised lots of exercises and mocks, you should be well prepared for the exam.

However, it is still important to have a carefully planned and thought through strategy to cope with those three hours of exam time.

This chapter takes you through some of the key skills to master to ensure all your careful preparation does not go to waste.

2 Importance of time management

Someone once referred to case study exams as "the race against time" and it's difficult to imagine a more accurate description. Being able to do what the examiner is wanting is only half of the battle; being able to deliver it in the time available is another matter altogether. This is even more important than in previous exams you may have faced because each section in the real exam is now timed and that once that time is up you will be moved on. Case study is not like a traditional exam where you can go back to a question if you get extra inspiration or feel you have some time left over. You have to complete each task within the time stated.

For this reason, time management is a key skill required to pass the Case Study Examination.

Successful time management requires two things:

- A tailored time plan – one that plays to your personal strengths and weaknesses; and

- Discipline in order to stick to it!

Time robbers

There are a number of ways in which time can be wasted or not used effectively in the Case Study Examination. An awareness of these will help to ensure you don't waste time in your exam.

Inactive reading

The first part of each task must be spent actively reading, processing the information and considering the impact on the organisation, how the issues link together and what could be done to resolve them. You may not have time to have a second detailed read and so these thoughts must be captured first time around.

Too much time spent on presentation

You will be writing your answer in software with some similarities to Microsoft Word however the only functions available are

- Cut

- Copy

- Paste

- Undo

- Redo

- Bold

- Italic

- Underline

While there are no specific marks for presentation, candidates need to be mindful that the better presented the answer is in terms of headings, sub-headings and so on, the easier the job will be for the marker. So, presentation is important, but not to the point of wasting time using fancy formatting for its own sake.

Being a perfectionist

Students can often spend such a long time pondering about what to write that over the course of a 3 hour exam, over half of it is spent staring into space.

As you are sitting a computer exam you not only spend time pondering, but also have the ability to delete so can change your mind several times before settling on the right word combinations. Just focus on getting your points down and don't worry about whether they could have been phrased better.

Although do bear in mind that the marker has to be able to read and understand your answer, so do write in clear English.

Too much detail on earlier parts of the requirement

As we've said earlier, not finishing answers is a key reason for failing the Case Study Examination. One of the main reasons why students fail to finish a section is a lack of discipline when writing about an issue. They feel they have to get all of their points down rather than selecting the better points and moving on. If a task requires you to discuss three different areas it is vital that you cover all parts adequately.

Too much correction

Often students can reread paragraphs three or more times before they move on to writing the next part of their answer. Instead, try to leave the read through until the final few minutes of the task and try to correct as many obvious errors as possible. The CIMA marker will be reading and marking your script on screen and it is harder to read and understand the points you are making if there are many typing errors.

3   Assimilation of information

One of the most challenging things to deal with in a case study examination is the volume of information which you have available. This is particularly difficult when you have both pre-seen and unseen information to manage and draw from. It is important that you refer to relevant pre-seen information in your responses as well as incorporating the unseen information.

The key things that you need to do to assimilate the information effectively and efficiently are:

- Read about and identify each event

- Consider what the issue is

- Evaluate the impact of the issue. Who is affected, by how much are they affected and what would happen if no action was taken?

- Determine the most useful and relevant exhibits from the pre-seen

Capturing all of your thoughts and ideas at this stage can be difficult and time consuming.

The following section on planning your answer will show you how to do this effectively without wasting time or effort.

4   Planning your answers

In section 2 of this chapter we saw how important it was to manage your time in the exam to ensure you're able to complete all of the necessary stages in the preparation of your answer.

One important aspect of your exam is planning your answer. Sitting the Case Study Exam is not as straight forward as turning up, reading the requirements, and then writing your answer.

If you do attempt to write without any form of content plan, your response will lack direction and a logical flow, it won't fully address the key points required and any recommendations will lack solid justification. It is for this reason that time should be specifically allocated to planning the content of your answers.

Given the preparation you've done before the exam, reading the unseen can often feel like a firework display is happening in your brain; each new piece of information you read about triggers a series of thoughts and ideas.

The planning process must therefore begin as soon as you start reading the unseen information. Every second counts within the case study exam and so it's important to use all of your time effectively by capturing the thoughts as they come to you.

To make sure the time spent now is of use to you throughout the task, you will need consider carefully how best to document your thoughts. You will be provided with an on-screen notes page ('scratchpad') as well as a wipe-clean laminated notes page and marker pen. Any method you adopt to plan must be concise whilst still allowing you to capture all of your ideas and see the bigger picture in terms of how the issues interrelate with one another.

Furthermore, the method must suit you! Everyone is different and what might work for one person could be a disaster for another. For example, some people prefer to work with lists, others with mind maps.

Most people find that some form of central planning sheet (to enable the bigger picture to be seen) is best. How you prepare the central planning sheet is a matter of personal preference and we've given illustrations of two different methods below. Practise each one to find out which you prefer and then tailor it further to settle on something that works for you.

Method 1 – planning within the answer box (highly recommended!)

This process is ideally suited to people who prefer lists and structure and is most easily done within the answer box using the exam software.

Step 1:

- Begin by reading everything in the task exhibit

- Ensure you have identified all aspects of the requirements, paying particular attention to the verbs used, and then write the requirements out as headings and sub headings within your answer box.

  For example, if asked to evaluate a proposal, then you would want arguments for and against, so these could be added as sub-headings at the very start.

- Brainstorm how you would answer the task, bringing in technical knowledge.

  For example, if deciding whether to close down a gym, you could jot down "use relevant costing".

Step 2:

- Read everything in the wider exhibit and associated reference materials, making notes under the relevant task headings and sub-headings.

  For example, if asked to explain why a sales mix variance is adverse, then you may find that the examiner has already given you two specific operational issues within the exam that can be addressed in your answer.

Step 3:

- Review your notes and headings to identify any linkages to information provided in the pre-seen and note under the relevant heading.

Step 4:

- Convert your rough notes into a finished answer.

- This will involve a mixture of deleting some points, developing others and in some cases, generating new ideas under headings that are lacking. The beauty of the word processor is that things can be deleted or expanded upon very easily.

Method 2 – The extended mind map

This process is ideally suited to those who prefer pictures and diagrams to trigger their thoughts.

Step 1:

- Read the unseen information and identify the key tasks required

- As you read, write each task in a "bubble" on your wipe-clean laminated notes page.

Step 2:

- Keep adding each new part of the task you identify to your sheet. At the end you should have a page with a number of bubbles dotted about.

Step 3:

- Review your bubbles to identify any linkages to the trigger information or pre-seen exhibits. Add any relevant information to your planning sheet in a bubble attached to the appropriate part of the task.

Step 4:

- Review the task bubbles and brainstorm any relevant knowledge which you can use in responding to the task. Add this to bubbles attached to the task.

With detailed information provided in the exam it would be very likely that your brain would think of a wide range of ideas which, if left uncaptured, would be forgotten as quickly as you thought of them.

This is where mind mapping comes in handy. You would not of course need to draw one as neat as this and feel free to add colours or graphics to help your thought processes.

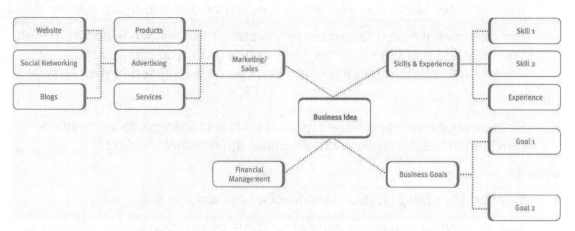

Have a go!

Some additional guidance

(1)   This is perhaps the hardest part of the exam; as soon as you tell your brain it needs to come up with some ideas, it very often refuses to cooperate! Practice makes perfect so working through the exercises in Chapter 6 and attempting mock exams will really help your brain to deliver ideas when you need it to.

(2)   Don't simply view technical models as something that must be included to tick a box if explicitly requested in the requirements. Instead use the models to help analyse the issues, suggest solutions or generate ideas. They were developed to be useful!

(3)   If you start looking at one of the task requirements and are stuck for ideas, don't waste time staring into space. Move on to the next part of the task (but not onto the next task itself as you won't be able to return) and you'll find the creative juices soon start flowing.

5   Presentation and communication

The Case Study examinations aim to test a wide range of skills and you may be required to communicate in many different ways to various different audiences, each with different information needs. In the exam, you will be given a blank answer box with no headings, so you need to ensure that you include the basic presentation elements required as shown below. However, rather than worrying about different formats in excessive detail, the key is to communicate clearly so that the marker can understand what you are saying.

An email

A requirement to draft an email may be in response to a specific question raised by an individual within the unseen information, or perhaps even in response to an email that is presented within the unseen.

 Illustration 1 – Email

In the real world, a typical layout for an email would be:

Email	
To:	Finance Director
From:	Finance Officer
Date:	Today
Subject:	RE ....
Content…	

However, in the exam, there are no marks for such headings, so it is more important to focus on the content of your response. If you are asked to write an email, then you should write short sentences (the number of which may well be specified in the requirement) that directly address the requirements.

A report

In the exam a commonly requested format is a report. Alternatively, you might also be asked for sections of a report and not the whole thing.

Illustration 2 – Report

In the real world, a typical layout for a report would be:

Title: A report on the implementation of Total Quality Management

Introduction

Brief background/context for requirement

Main report content broken down using further sub-headings

Conclusion

Key conclusions and recommendations

However, with a report, an introduction and conclusion/ recommendation is probably not advised as this could just waste time. The key thing always is that you answer all aspects of the question clearly and logically with headings. At the operational level you don't need to waste time with formal report structures.

Slide presentation

If a slide presentation is called for, your answer need only consist of the bullet points that would appear on each slide. Read the requirement carefully as guidance will be given on how many slides to prepare and the maximum number of bullets on each slide. Most likely this would be 2 slides, with a maximum of 5 bullets on each slide (or you may just be asked for 10 bullet points in total).

Illustration 3 – Slides

A typical layout for the presentation of slides would be:

Slide 1

Title

- XX
- XX
- XX
- XX
- XX

You will not need to prepare speaker notes.

As with emails, do not worry too much about presentation – you do not need to layout your answer as a slide (e.g. you don't need to draw a box). Simply using the heading "Slide 1" and noting the bullets will be sufficient.

A letter

Exactly the same as for an email but laid out in letter format. That means you should include a space for an address, a date, state to whom the letter is addressed and a summary of what the letter is regarding.

The letter should be signed off in the normal business fashion, unless you are told otherwise.

Illustration 4 – Letter

A typical layout for the presentation of a letter should be:

> **Address**
>
> **Date**
>
> **Dear X**
>
> **Title**
>
> Content of your answer to the requirement using short sentences or bullet points as instructed.
>
> Yours sincerely,
>
> A Management Accountant

---

6 Writing style

Introduction

Writing style is something that develops over time. It is influenced by your education and experiences. To some it comes easily, they enjoy words – but remember, you are not looking to win any prizes in literature. It's about putting facts, ideas and opinions in a clear, concise, logical fashion. Some students get very worried about their writing styles. As a general rule you should try to write as you would talk.

Logical flow

A typical point starts with a statement of fact, either given in the case or derived from analysis – 'what?'

This can then be followed by an interpretation – 'so what?'

This can then lead to an implication – 'now what?', or 'what next?'

For example:

(1) What? – The net relevant cash flow for the project is positive.

(2) So what? – Suggesting we should go ahead with the project.

(3) Now what? – Arrange board meeting to discuss strategic implications.

A similar structure can be obtained using the Socratic approach – what, why, how?

- So what?

- Why should we use it?

- How does it work?

Who is reading the response?

Failure to pitch the level correctly will inevitably result in failure to communicate your ideas effectively, since the reader will either be swamped with complexity, or bored with blandness. The recipients of the report should also dictate the level of tact required.

Tactless	Tactful
The directors have clearly made errors	There were other options open to the board that, with hindsight, would have been beneficial
The marketing director is responsible for this disastrous change in strategy	The board should consider where this went wrong? It would appear that the marketing department may have made some mistakes

Making your response easy to read

To ensure that the marker finds your answers accessible and easy to read, you should try to do the following:

- Use short words, short sentences, short phrases and short paragraphs. If you are adopting the 'what, so what, what now' approach, then you could have a paragraph containing three sentences. The next point can then be a new paragraph, also containing three sentences.

- Use the correct words to explain what you mean! For example, students often get confused between:

  - recommendations (what they should do – actions) and options (what they could do – possibilities).

  - objectives (what we want to achieve – the destination) and strategies (how we intend to achieve them – the route).

- Avoid using vague generalisations. Too often students will comment that an issue will "impact" on profit rather than being specific about whether profit will increase or decrease (or even better still, trying to quantify by how much). Other common phrases which are too vague include "communicate with" (you need to say specifically what should be discussed) and "look in to" (how should an option be looked in to?)

- Avoid unnecessary repetition. This can either be of information from the exam paper (pre-seen or unseen), of discussion within the report (in particular between what is said in one section and another) or can relate to the words that you use.

Some students fall into the trap of thinking that writing a professional report means simply writing more words to say the same thing! The issue is quality not quantity.

For example, compare the following:

- 'I, myself, personally' OR 'I'

- 'export overseas' OR 'export'

- 'green in colour' OR 'green'

- Watch your spelling – this may seem a small and unimportant point, but poor spelling makes a document seem sloppy and may convey an impression that the content is as loose as the general appearance! Poor spelling interrupts the marker as they read your report, so there is the danger that they conclude that it did not have a logical flow.

- Recommendations – be decisive – do not 'sit on the fence' or ask for more information. Make a clear recommendation based on the information you have and justify why you have chosen that course of action.

Exercise 1

This exercise will get you thinking about what makes a well written script. The technical content of the requirement is not relevant – we are focusing on writing style and flow.

> The risk committee of X plc met to discuss a report by its risk manager. The report focused on a number of risks that applied to a chemicals factory recently acquired in another country.
>
> She explained that the new risks related to the security of the new factory in respect of burglary, the supply of one of the key raw materials that experienced fluctuations in world supply and also an environmental risk.
>
> The environmental risk was with respect to the possibility of poisonous emissions from the new factory. The CEO who chaired the risk committee, said that the factory was important to him for two reasons. First, he said it was strategically important to the company. Second, it was important because his own bonuses depended upon it. He said that he knew from the report what the risks were, but that he wanted somebody to explain to him what strategies they could use to manage the risks. 'I don't get any bonus at all until we reach a high level of output from the factory,' he said. 'So I don't care what the risks are, we will have to manage them.'

You have been asked to outline strategies that can be used to manage risk and identify, with reasons, an appropriate strategy for each of the three risks facing the new venture.

Requirement:

Consider these two responses and note the positive and negative aspects of each.

Answer 1

Introduction

Risk can be managed using the following strategies.

- **Transfer** the risk to another organisation for example by buying insurance. This is usually cost effective where the probability of the risk is low but the impact is potentially high.

- **Avoid** the risk altogether by withdrawing completely from the risky activity. This is done where the risk is high probability and high frequency and so it is too costly to reduce the risk sufficiently.

- **Reduce** the risk by implementing controls or by diversification.

- **Accept** the risk without taking any further steps to mitigate it. For this to be acceptable the frequency and the impact of the risk must place the risk within the risk appetite of the company.

Risk of burglary

It is usual to insure against burglary an example of the transfer strategy. This is because of the high impact of burglary.

It is also usual to put safeguards in place such as security guards because of the probability of burglary. This is an example of risk reduction.

Raw materials supply fluctuation

Depending on the cost benefit analysis the company could chose to transfer the risk by entering into forward contracts to purchase the materials.

There will be a cost associated with this and it will lower but not remove the risk associated with supply and price fluctuations. They may choose to accept the risk as part of the operational risk associated with their industry.

Environmental risk

The company should take reasonable steps to reduce the chance poisonous emissions. It should use appropriate technology and controls to reduce the risk.

Risks cannot be completely eliminated so if the poisonous emissions could give rise to significant costs it should also purchase insurance and transfer the risk.

7 Summary

You should have an appreciation of some of the issues you may encounter in the exam and some possible techniques to overcome these.

Next steps:

(1) In the next two chapters we will present the unseen and guide you through the process of producing an answer. It is worth ensuring you can log on to the Pearson Vue site now and make sure you have registered for the practice case study exam. It is advisable to familiarise yourself with the software as much as possible.

(2) As you are about to embark on a full attempt at the "question tutorial" paper it is a good time to revisit previous chapters and ensure you are comfortable with all of the material so far before proceeding.

Test your understanding answers

Exercise 1

The first solution has several positive aspects:

- Brief introduction linking to requirement
- Overview of model with explanation and clear examples
- Specific points from scenario addressed
- Headings clearly signpost the answer
- Appropriate language

There are some areas which could be improved:

- Specific reference to the company name
- More explicit use of the information from the scenario

The second solution is not as strong as the first. Some of the main criticisms:

- Main options available are not clearly explained
- No attempt to introduce the answer
- Inappropriate language for a formal report/response
- Lack of tact regarding the CEO – the intended audience!!

As a piece of writing there is not much to say from a positive perspective except:

- Clear structure
- Writing is concise (but probably a bit too brief)

2019 Prototype exam – walkthrough of variant 1

Chapter learning objectives

- To gain experience trying to answer a case study exam.

1 The aim of a walkthrough

The aim of this chapter is to give you a chance to practise many of the techniques you have been shown in previous chapters of this study text. This should help you to understand the various thought processes needed to complete the full three hour examination. It is important that you work through this chapter at a steady pace.

Don't rush on to the next stage until you have properly digested the information, followed the guidance labelled 'Stop and Think!' and made your own notes. This will give you more confidence than simply reading the model solutions. You should refer to the unseen produced in the previous chapter as you proceed through these exercises.

2 First screen

The opening screen of the exam shows you how many sub-tasks you have to deal with and how to allocate your time within tasks:

Section (task)	Time for section (minutes)	Number of answer screens	Number of sub-tasks	% time to spend on each sub-task
1	45	1	2	(a) 48% (b) 52%
2	45	1	2	(a) 52% (b) 48%
3	45	1	2	(a) 36% (b) 64%
4	45	1	2	(a) 60% (b) 40%

The exam software will prevent you from spending more than 45 minutes on task 4, say, but you need to ensure that this is split 27 minutes on sub-task (a) and 18 minutes on sub-task (b)

3 Task 1

Understanding the context

The first screen of task 1 reveals that GymFit has purchased Fit4Life's gym portfolio:

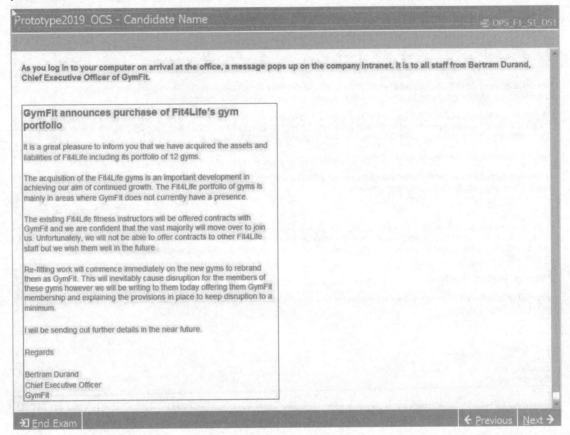

Stop and think!

(1) Start thinking about the relevant information in the pre-seen. It's very important that your responses are applied to the scenario. For example, how much can you remember about Fit4Life? We were told in the pre-seen that

"The rising star in the Celtland market is Fit4Life which has ruthlessly marketed itself as a lifelong alternative to the other low-cost gyms. Fit4Life offers members a lifelong membership fee which will not increase provided the customer remains a member. Its rapid growth has also been driven by its use of specialised fitness apps which have been developed using data analytics. These apps provide members with tailored personal training advice and programmes which they can access at home"

(2) GymFit is acquiring the assets and liabilities, not buying the company – group accounting is not in the F1 syllabus.

(3) There could be integration issues relating such as rebranding but also HR issues (E1) relating to existing staff moving over to GymFit

Answering the question set – understanding the requirements

The requirements (and further context) are given on the next screen:

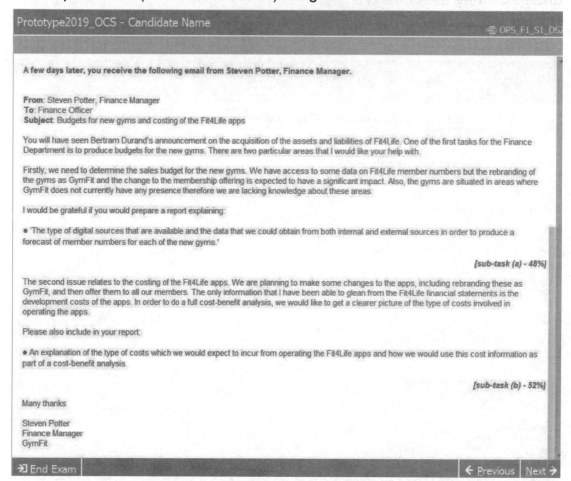

It is vital that you understand the nature and scope of the requirements. Here you need to prepare a report which covers:

- "The type of digital sources that are available and the data that we could obtain from both internal and external sources in order to produce a forecast of member numbers for each of the new gyms"

    Make sure you answer the question set – we need to cover both **internal** and **external** sources but are only asked for forecasts for the **new** gyms (i.e. those previously owned by Fit4Life), not our existing gyms. Similarly we only want data that will specifically help us estimate membership **numbers,** not to forecast how much they typically spend, for example.

- "An explanation of the types of cost which we would expect to incur from operating the Fit4life apps and how we would use this information as part of a cost-benefit analysis."

    "To **explain**" is a higher level verb that "to list". You need to make clear further details about the costs – what is a 'digital' source, why this cost will arise and/or how it behaves and/or even try to quantify it.

    Separately you need to explain how each one would be used in CBA in the **context** of the decision to rebrand the apps.

Let's plan – Task 1(a)

If you prefer to plan within your answer box, then the above considerations will help you set up suitable headings and then start to populate them.

Alternatively, if you prefer to use your wipe clean whiteboard, then you could split your planning sheet into a grid to ensure all parts are covered:

Type of source	Data GymFit could obtain
External	
Internal	

Either way, you now need to brainstorm all the relevant points you can think of under the above headings, making sure you are bringing together your knowledge from the relevant syllabus as well as your analysis of the pre-seen information.

Let's think a bit more about these requirements by breaking them down into the component parts.

External sources – from your E1 studies you will know that secondary research can include looking at government reports on population and incomes, industry reports, websites and so on. The task does hint at looking at different "areas", so start with these.

Internal sources – we are told that we would have Fit4All membership lists in order to email them and offer GymFit memberships but you could also think about existing GymFit data that could help as well, such as membership numbers for similar sized gyms in similar areas (e.g. near towns or business parks)

It is vital that each source has a corresponding comment on what information could be obtained and how this could help forecast membership numbers.

Task 1(b)

Again you could set up headings within your answer or use a planning sheet:

Type of cost	Use within CBA

From your P1 knowledge, you will be aware that digital products, such as apps, have a wide range of cost types, including IT support and infrastructure costs, and that the timing and frequency of costs will be difficult to estimate. Try to apply as many of your comments as possible to the fact we are talking about an app, rather than a manufacturer of baked beans!

As a rough rule of thumb you should spend about 15–20% of the time available for reading and planning. So for this section of the exam, where you are given 45 minutes, you should be spending approximately 7–8 minutes planning your answer before you complete the exercise below. This would leave you about 35 minutes to write your answer and a few minutes spare to check through what you have written.

Exercise 1

Prepare a response to the first task in the prototype exam GymFit.

4 Task 2

For task 2, the trigger and requirements are mixed together into one screen, together with reference material:

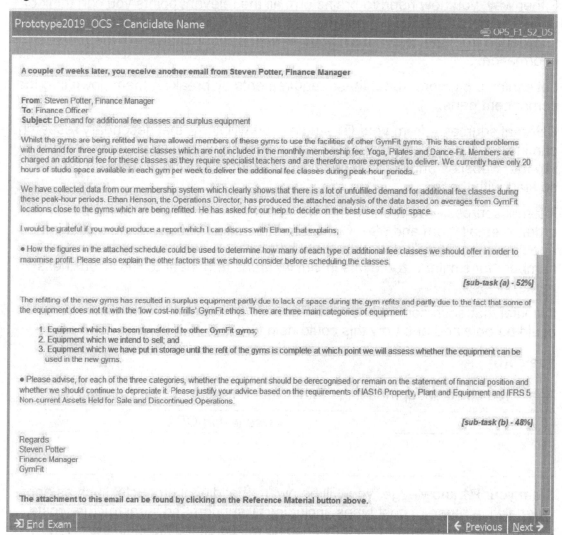

Prototype2019_OCS - Candidate Name   OPS_F1_S2_DS

A couple of weeks later, you receive another email from Steven Potter, Finance Manager

From: Steven Potter, Finance Manager
To: Finance Officer
Subject: Demand for additional fee classes and surplus equipment

Whilst the gyms are being refitted we have allowed members of these gyms to use the facilities of other GymFit gyms. This has created problems with demand for three group exercise classes which are not included in the monthly membership fee: Yoga, Pilates and Dance-Fit. Members are charged an additional fee for these classes as they require specialist teachers and are therefore more expensive to deliver. We currently have only 20 hours of studio space available in each gym per week to deliver the additional fee classes during peak-hour periods.

We have collected data from our membership system which clearly shows that there is a lot of unfulfilled demand for additional fee classes during these peak-hour periods. Ethan Henson, the Operations Director, has produced the attached analysis of the data based on averages from GymFit locations close to the gyms which are being refitted. He has asked for our help to decide on the best use of studio space.

I would be grateful if you would produce a report which I can discuss with Ethan, that explains;

• How the figures in the attached schedule could be used to determine how many of each type of additional fee classes we should offer in order to maximise profit. Please also explain the other factors that we should consider before scheduling the classes.

[sub-task (a) - 52%]

The refitting of the new gyms has resulted in surplus equipment partly due to lack of space during the gym refits and partly due to the fact that some of the equipment does not fit with the 'low cost-no frills' GymFit ethos. There are three main categories of equipment:

  1. Equipment which has been transferred to other GymFit gyms;
  2. Equipment which we intend to sell; and
  3. Equipment which we have put in storage until the refit of the gyms is complete at which point we will assess whether the equipment can be used in the new gyms.

• Please advise, for each of the three categories, whether the equipment should be derecognised or remain on the statement of financial position and whether we should continue to depreciate it. Please justify your advice based on the requirements of IAS16 Property, Plant and Equipment and IFRS 5 Non-current Assets Held for Sale and Discontinued Operations.

[sub-task (b) - 48%]

Regards
Steven Potter
Finance Manager
GymFit

The attachment to this email can be found by clicking on the Reference Material button above.

End Exam   ← Previous   Next →

Understanding the context

With tasks like this, you still need to appreciate the bigger context before launching into the specific requirements. Within the context of refurbishment, we have (a) decision making under constraints and (b) FR advice.

Stop and think!

(1) Using your P1 knowledge, consider how should they allocate scarce studio time (profit, contribution, contribution per hour, throughput...)?

(2) You won't be expected to do complicated calculations, so what you need should already have been done for you in the reference materials:

Analysis of contribution from additional fee classes during peak-hour periods			
	Yoga	Pilates	Dance-Fit
Class capacity limit (number of participants)	15	15	20
Class length (hours)	1.50	1.00	0.75
Estimated demand per week (number of members)	150	90	80
Number of classes required per week	10	6	4
Number of hours required per week	15	6	3
Contribution per hour	C$35.00	C$45.00	C$65.00
Contribution per class	C$52.50	C$45.00	C$48.75

(3) Can you remember the financial reporting rules for which assets should be recognised / derecognised and the implications for depreciation?

Answering the question set – understanding the requirements

Given the above, the specific requirements are worded as follows:

"Produce a report ... that explains

- "How the figures in the attached appendix could be used to determine how many of each type of additional fee classes we should offer in order to maximise profit. Please also explain the other factors that we should consider before scheduling the classes."

  Note that you need to explain **how** the numbers will be used – i.e. explain the **methodology**, not just get to the right answer. Also you are asked for **other** factors.

- "Please advise, for each of the three categories, whether the equipment should be derecognised or remain on the statement of financial position and whether we should continue to depreciate it. Please justify your advice based on the requirements of IAS16 Property, Plant and Equipment and IFRS5 Non-current assets Held for sale and Discontinued Operations."

  Note that there are two elements here – should the assets be **derecognised** and should we continue to **depreciate** them.

Let's plan!

Task 2(a)

For P1 methodology type tasks the following approach is useful:

- **Explain** the method – why do you use contribution, why are fixed costs excluded, what is the scarce resource, how are products ranked (contribution per unit of scarce resource) and how is the resource then allocated?

- **Apply** the method – walk through the steps above applying them to the specific context – what is the scarce resource here, which class would be prioritised first, how much time does this use up, how much is left for the second choice and so on?

- **Go beyond** the method and discuss wider issues – here you are asked for "other factors" but previous tasks have asked for limitations, extra information required and so on.

Task 2(b)

For F1 financial reporting tasks use the following steps:

- **Identify** the relevant standards / topics – here we are told to use IAS 16 and IFRS5 and are given assets in 3 categories – those to be transferred, those held for sale and those where the future is unclear. The requirement emphasises whether assets should be derecognised and whether GymFit should continue to depreciate them.

- **State** the rules – for example, outline the criteria that have to be met for assets to be classified as "held for sale" and the implications for the financial statements if they are so classified.

- **Apply** the rules to the specific context – for example, do any of the assets held by GymFit meet the criteria for assets "held for sale"? If so, then what are the specific consequences?

Exercise 2
Prepare a response to the second task.

5 Task 3

As for task 2, the trigger and requirements for task 3 are mixed together into one screen, together with reference material:

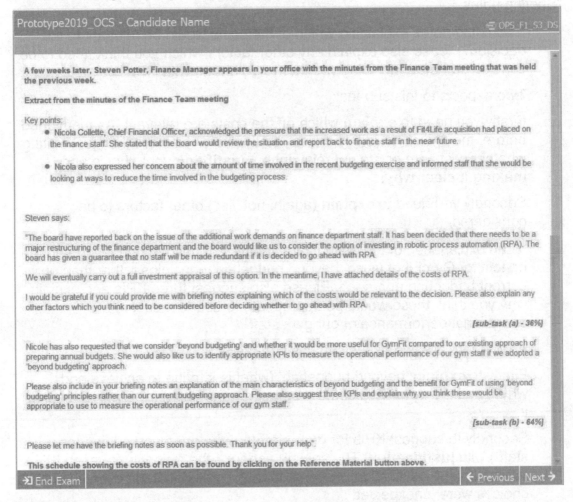

Understanding the context

The acquisition has highlighted the need to improve the way the finance function operates. Suggested improvements are investment into RPA and a switch to beyond budgeting. Here the context is E1 based (the operation of the finance function) but the specific requirements are more P1 focussed (relevant costing and budgeting).

Also note the specific problems highlighted as you will want to ensure that you address these in your answer:

- **Pressure** that the increased workload has placed on staff

- The **time** involved in the recent budgeting exercise

Stop and think!

- Can you remember the principles of relevant costing and the characteristics, pros and cons of 'beyond budgeting' from P1?

- Can you remember the pros and cons of RPA from E1?

Answering the question set – understanding the requirements

The requirements are worded as follows:

"Briefing notes…"

- "…briefing notes explaining which of the costs would be relevant to the decision. Please also explain any other factors which you think need to be considered before deciding whether to go ahead with RPA"

Two aspects to this sub-task.

Firstly you need to **explain** which off the costs are relevant. As mentioned before, the choice of verb is critical, so this involves more than just stating whether costs are or are not relevant but **justifying** your choice and **making it clear why**.

Secondly you need to **explain** (again, not 'list') other factors to be considered.

- "…an explanation of the main characteristics of beyond budgeting and the benefit for GymFit of using 'beyond budgeting' principles rather than our current budgeting approach. Please also suggest three KPIs and explain why you think these would be appropriate to use to measure the operational performance of our gym staff".

Again there are two aspects to this sub-task.

Firstly to **explain** 'beyond budgeting' (what is it trying to achieve and why?) and the **benefit** (just the pros but not the cons) for GymFit of using it.

Secondly to suggest KPIs for **gym** staff (not the over-worked finance staff!) with **justification**. The second aspect – the rationale for each KPI – is vital. If your justification is strong, then you still get credit even if your choices were 'unexpected'.

Let's plan!

Task 3(a)

As stated in the commentary on task 2, for P1 methodology type tasks the following approach is useful:

- **Explain** the method – briefly explain what we mean by 'relevant costs' (future, incremental cash flows)

- **Apply** the method – walk through the costs in the reference materials line by line and explain how the rules apply to each specific cost.

Robot Process Automation (RPA)		
Cost categories	C$	Notes
Depreciation and amortisation of hardware / software	(10,000)	(1)
Amortisation of development costs	(15,000)	(2)
IT maintenance costs	(37,000)	(3)
Licence fees	(8,000)	(4)
Staff training costs	(10,000)	(5)
Total costs	(80,000)	
Savings on salaries and benefits	120,000	(6)
Net benefit	40,000	

Notes:
1. The depreciation and amortisation of hardware and software is based on the assumption that the transaction processing operations will require two robots.
2. The development costs relate to the planning, assessment, design and testing of the RPA.
3. The IT maintenance costs relate to the costs of an existing employees who will be responsible for maintenance of the hardware and updates to the software.
4. Licence fees are payable to the provider of the software for the robots.
5. Staff training will be required for existing accounting and IT staff.
6. Savings on salaries and benefits relate to the expected cost savings from not having to hire additional accounting staff.

End Exam   ← Previous | Next →

- **Go beyond** the method and discuss wider issues – here you are asked for "other factors" concerning the investment in RPA. Your comments can be derived from a number of sources:

  - The scenario (i.e. Will it reduce the pressure on finance staff? Will it speed up budgeting?),

  - From your P1 knowledge (e.g. relevant costing only includes factors that can be quantified in financial terms – what about non-financial issues such as staff morale?)

  - From your E1 knowledge – what are the pros and cons of RPA?

  With all of the above try to apply your comments to GymFit as much as possible.

Task 3(b)

The same answer approach to 3(a) can be applied here:

- **Explain** the method – briefly explain the characteristics of 'beyond budgeting'

- **Apply** the method – the key aspect here is whether GymFit should switch from its current method. Beyond budgeting is great for some organisations but not others – which of these categories does GymFit fit into and why?

- **Go beyond** the method and discuss wider issues – here this is incorporated into the "apply" stage.

In terms of the KPIs you are only asked for three, so focus on what you think the key operational staffing issues are for a gym. For example, you may feel that quality is important (explain why!) and that one way of measuring this would be by looking at the number of customer complaints.

Exercise 3
Prepare a response to the third task.

6   Task 4

As for tasks 2 and 3, the trigger and requirements for task 4 are mixed together into one screen, together with reference material:

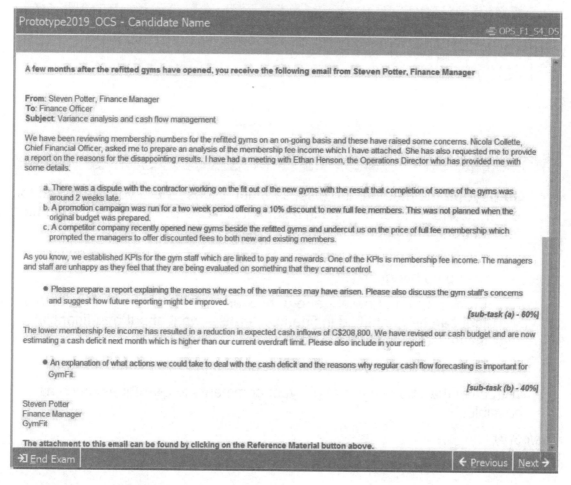

Prototype2019_OCS - Candidate Name   ☰ OPS_F1_S4_DS

A few months after the refitted gyms have opened, you receive the following email from Steven Potter, Finance Manager

From: Steven Potter, Finance Manager
To: Finance Officer
Subject: Variance analysis and cash flow management

We have been reviewing membership numbers for the refitted gyms on an on-going basis and these have raised some concerns. Nicola Collette, Chief Financial Officer, asked me to prepare an analysis of the membership fee income which I have attached. She has also requested me to provide a report on the reasons for the disappointing results. I have had a meeting with Ethan Henson, the Operations Director who has provided me with some details.

    a. There was a dispute with the contractor working on the fit out of the new gyms with the result that completion of some of the gyms was around 2 weeks late.
    b. A promotion campaign was run for a two week period offering a 10% discount to new full fee members. This was not planned when the original budget was prepared.
    c. A competitor company recently opened new gyms beside the refitted gyms and undercut us on the price of full fee membership which prompted the managers to offer discounted fees to both new and existing members.

As you know, we established KPIs for the gym staff which are linked to pay and rewards. One of the KPIs is membership fee income. The managers and staff are unhappy as they feel that they are being evaluated on something that they cannot control.

    ● Please prepare a report explaining the reasons why each of the variances may have arisen. Please also discuss the gym staff's concerns and suggest how future reporting might be improved.

                                                     [sub-task (a) - 60%]

The lower membership fee income has resulted in a reduction in expected cash inflows of C$208,800. We have revised our cash budget and are now estimating a cash deficit next month which is higher than our current overdraft limit. Please also include in your report:

    ● An explanation of what actions we could take to deal with the cash deficit and the reasons why regular cash flow forecasting is important for GymFit.

                                                     [sub-task (b) - 40%]

Steven Potter
Finance Manager
GymFit

The attachment to this email can be found by clicking on the Reference Material button above.

⇥ End Exam   ← Previous | Next →

Understanding the context

It is now a few months' later and membership numbers have been disappointing, giving rise to a number of adverse sales variances and poor results on KPIs that link to staff pay and rewards. Staff concerns over the controllability of a specific KPI – membership fee income – are highlighted.

Furthermore, this has also resulted in cash flow problems that may mean the overdraft limit will be breached.

Three operational factors are highlighted that will give key context for aspects of your answer:

- A dispute with a contractor

- An unplanned promotional campaign

- Activities of a competitor

Stop and think!

- You will not be expected to calculate variances but can you remember the ideas behind sales mix and quantity variances and possible causes for them from P1?

- Using knowledge from P1 and E1, can you remember the issues around setting staff targets that they feel are not fully controllable by them and the implications for motivation?

- How many ways of addressing a cash deficit can you remember from F1?

Answering the question set – understanding the requirements

The requirements are worded as follows:

- "Please prepare a report explaining the reasons why each of the variances may have arisen. Please also discuss the gym staff's concerns and suggest how future reporting may be improved".

  You have to **explain** why each of three variances have arisen, meaning that simple list of generic factors and causes is not sufficient. Your answer must make it clear the likely causes in this case.

  You are then asked to **discuss** staff concerns. In order to discuss something, there normally needs to be an 'argument' with opposing viewpoints. Also, any discussion should, if possible, end in a conclusion. In this context the discussion is whether or not the staff concerns are valid. A good answer does not simply say "yes" or "no" but considers both sides of the argument and the extent to which it can it be said that the KPI of membership fee income is in or out of their control.

  Finally you have to **suggest** how reporting could be improved. The verb here would indicate that in-depth justification is not required (but some helps!)

- "An explanation of what actions we could take to deal with the cash deficit and the reasons why regular cash flow forecasting is important for GymFit".

  As with previous tasks the verb used here is "to **explain**", so your answer needs more than just a list of options. Try to apply your comments to the context and ensure they are worded as **actions** GymFit could take.

  Finally, you have to explain the reasons why regular cash flow forecasting is important for GymFit, so it is vital that your answers moves beyond generic reasons why cash budgeting is useful to specific reasons for GymFit, such as the fact that it has allowed us to anticipate breaching the overdraft limit, so action can be taken to avoid that outcome.

Let's plan!

Task 4(a)

With variance tasks such as this the following approach is useful:

- Briefly explain what each variance **means**. For example, an adverse price variance means that actual fees paid per customer per month were lower than budgeted. (Aside: how would you explain the adverse sales mix variance?)

- For each of the variances given, look for possible **causes**:

   Start with the three given in the exam – do any of them apply here?

   Next examine any financial data given. While you don't have to perform calculations, you may spot key areas by looking at the numbers. For example, examining the reference materials:

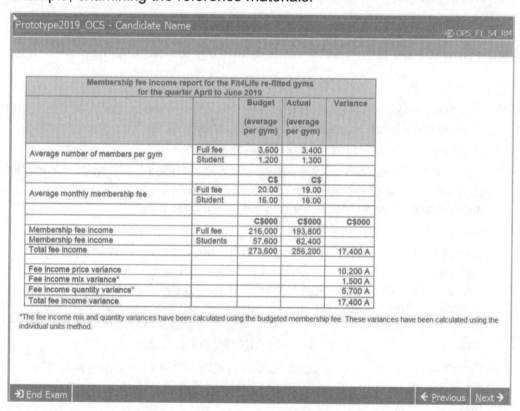

Membership fee income report for the Fit4Life re-fitted gyms for the quarter April to June 2019		Budget (average per gym)	Actual (average per gym)	Variance
Average number of members per gym	Full fee	3,600	3,400	
	Student	1,200	1,300	
		C$	C$	
Average monthly membership fee	Full fee	20.00	19.00	
	Student	16.00	16.00	
		C$000	C$000	C$000
Membership fee income	Full fee	216,000	193,800	
Membership fee income	Students	57,600	62,400	
Total fee income		273,600	256,200	17,400 A
Fee income price variance				10,200 A
Fee income mix variance*				1,500 A
Fee income quantity variance*				5,700 A
Total fee income variance				17,400 A

*The fee income mix and quantity variances have been calculated using the budgeted membership fee. These variances have been calculated using the individual units method.

We can see that the actual price for students is the same as the budgeted figure, so any price variance is purely due to full fee members.

Can you remember anything in the pre-seen that might help? For example, the reference materials distinguish full fee and student members but GymFit also offers three types of membership – one gym, two gym and 'bundle' membership – is this relevant to the variances?

As stated above, when discussing the staff concerns over KPIs you need to consider both sides of the argument, so you could split your planning into factors staff can control, factors they cannot and those with partial control or influence.

In terms of recommendations, you can keep your answer very practical in terms of suggesting new KPIs and/or ways of reporting variances, such as splitting between planning and operating variances.

Task 4(b)

To improve cash flow you could start by brainstorming as many possible options as possible and then prioritising your list, so that you write about the 'best' ideas first. For example, suggesting that GymFit discuss the issue with their bank to arrange an overdraft extension should be discussed before, say, a share issue to raise long term funds.

Finally try to address specific concerns over why cash flow forecasting is important first, such as to manage the risk of exceeding the overdraft, before resorting to generic ideas, such as helping the company reduce its cost of finance.

Exercise 4
Prepare a response to the fourth task.

7 Summary

You should now have a better understanding of how to approach the exam requirements and plan your answer. Although this chapter uses the "question tutorial" exam as an example, the techniques used can be applied to any set of exam tasks.

Next steps:

(1) As previously mentioned, you should attempt a written answer yourself to all of the tasks before reviewing the suggested solutions.

(2) Reviewing the solutions may highlight knowledge gaps which you may need to revisit.

(3) CIMA have produced two sample exams based on this pre-seen. You should try to attempt the second one at exam speed and using the exam software if possible.

Test your understanding answers

These answers have been provided by CIMA for information purposes only. The answers created are indicative of a response that could be given by a good candidate. They are not to be considered exhaustive, and other appropriate relevant responses would receive credit.

CIMA will not accept challenges to these answers on the basis of academic judgement.

Exercise 1

Digital sources and type of data

Digital sources are those that can be accessed by computers or other digital devices. Some of them are "born-digital," or originated in a digital form for example, pictures taken with a digital camera, web pages or twitter feeds, others were converted into digital files. Digital sources include e-books, e-journals, websites, blogs, online newspapers, online magazines and official government publications.

To determine the potential member numbers for each of the new gyms, we would need to establish the demographics of the local areas. This will involve accessing government statistics which will give us data on the size of the population within the local area. We know that the penetration rate for gym membership is 14.3% however that rate will vary depending on the demographics of the particular area. The government statistics will also provide us with further analysis of the population segmented by factors such as age; gender; income; disposable income; occupation and education level.

We can determine the profile of low-cost gym members from research reports which are available online. It is clear from previous research reports that the main determinants of gym membership are age; income and education level.

We can also access our membership database and, using data analytics, categorise our current membership. This will give us a better indication of the profile of the membership which is attracted by our current member proposition.

There will however be other factors that we would need to consider. Generally, gym members will live within 10 miles of the gym however a gym which is located close to an industrial area is likely to attract members from local businesses who will use the gym at lunchtime and after work. Access to good road or rail network may be an important factor in determining how far members may travel to access the gym. The proximity to a university may also be important in determining the mix of members between students and full fee members. The proximity of competitor gyms will also be a major factor in determining our member numbers.

All of these factors can be quantified by using data available via digital sources for example, government statistics or area maps.

Digital costing

Type of costs from operating Fit4Life apps

The cost of developing the apps whilst significant is not the only cost which needs to be considered. There are four main categories of costs associated with maintaining and operating apps post-development:

Functional services:

Functional services are those needed to execute the functionalities and features of the apps. While the apps developer will have provided a certain functionality, the apps will not work unless we subscribe to a service that will provide a delivery mechanism. This will allow functionality such as push notifications; social media and chat; SMS and email messaging.

Administrative services:

We will need an intuitive, powerful, accessible and user-friendly administration dashboard to enable us to effectively administer the apps. Administrative costs are the most difficult to anticipate as they will largely depend and differ based on each individual app. The administration dashboard will allow us to manage the content of the apps; manage the functional services detailed above; update the apps; manage user profiles; collect and analyse user behaviour; control access by users and enable data or user segmentation.

Infrastructure services:

These services include infrastructural components such as where the app is hosted, where data is stored and how the data is delivered. This will include the cost of servers (where the app is hosted); data storage; content delivery network (CDN) and images data.

IT support services:

Ongoing technical support is a critical component of any app deployment. We will need technical support to enable us to deal with iOS and Android updates; updates to application programming interfaces (APIs) and bug fixing. IT specific maintenance costs for infrastructure will also be required since servers, data storage, CDN and image data will all require some level of monitoring and maintenance.

Cost-benefit analysis

In order to carry out a cost-benefit analysis we will need to determine each of these costs and their frequency. Some of the cost will be paid regularly to suppliers such as the subscription costs associated with the apps' functionality. Other costs will require us to estimate the likelihood and extent of occurrence and the time involved with carrying out each task.

For example, we will need to estimate how often we will need to carry out iOS and Android updates or updates to APIs. Once we have established the time involved in each of these tasks, we can then determine the number of additional IT staff that would be required.

Some of the costs will be incurred on features or updates that are common to all the apps and an appropriate method will need to be determined to share the costs between the apps.

It will be necessary to establish the total costs over the lifetime of the app and then compare this to the expected benefits in terms of increased revenue. Determining the lifetime of an app can be very difficult particularly when there are rapid changes in technology as there is at the present time.

Exercise 2

Limiting factor analysis

How to use the figures in the schedule to decide on the mix of additional fee classes

The figures provided by Ethan could be used to determine the combination of classes which would maximise profit. It appears that time during peak periods is our scarce resource. It would require 24 hours to satisfy the demand for classes but only 20 hours are available. Ethan's analysis has provided contribution per class and contribution per hour for the three classes. Fixed costs are not considered since these would remain the same no matter which combination of classes are offered. Contribution per hour should be used to determine the optimum combination of classes since hours are the scarce resource and therefore we need to maximise the contribution from each hour.

In order to make a decision, we would rank the classes in descending order of contribution per hour and allocate the time available to satisfy the demand for the class that provides the highest contribution per hour first. Any remaining hours would be allocated to the class with the second highest contribution per hour. If any hours still remain, these would be used to satisfy as much as possible of the demand for the remaining class.

Dance-Fit is the top ranked class with C$65.00 contribution per hour and can be fully satisfied as only three hours of time are needed. Pilates has the second highest contribution per hour at C$45.00 and is therefore our second ranked class. Demand for Pilates classes can also be fully satisfied as these only require a further six hours. Yoga has the lowest contribution per hour at C$35.00 and therefore the remaining 12 hours would be used to run 8 Yoga classes.

Other factors to be considered

There are several other factors that could be considered which could potentially improve the decision. There are numerous assumptions and estimates contained in the analysis. It is possible, for example, that specialist teacher hours are also a constraint. There is an apparent assumption that there will be enough teacher availability but this may not be the case. It is also important to consider that demand is estimated and based on an average. Errors in the demand estimates could result in insufficient Dance-Fit or Pilates classes or even empty classes. It is also possible that some classes may not be full to capacity and this would change the contribution per hour. In addition, demand may vary for different locations and it would be better to make a decision based on the demand at each location.

We should also consider whether it is possible to increase capacity. There may be other larger studio spaces within each gym which could be used to reduce or remove the binding constraint. This could however potentially have consequences for the availability of places in the free classes. In addition, it may also be possible to change the length of the class. By reducing yoga to a one hour class, it may be possible to accommodate the vast majority of those who would like to take part in yoga.

We should also consider the impact of providing insufficient additional fee classes. This approach would leave insufficient provision for yoga, which could have significant implications for planned additional fee income in addition to customer satisfaction, retention and therefore membership income.

Financial accounting treatment of the surplus gym equipment

Equipment transferred to other gyms

The gym equipment is transferred to other gyms would remain on the statement of financial position under non-current assets and would continue to be depreciated in the normal way.

Equipment which we intend to sell

According to IFRS 5, non-current assets will be classified as 'assets held for sale' if their carrying amount will be recovered principally through a sales transaction rather than through continuing use.

In general, the following conditions must be met for an asset (or 'disposal group') to be classified as held for sale:

1 Management is committed to a plan to sell

2 The asset is available for immediate sale

3 An active programme to locate a buyer is initiated

4 The sale is highly probable, within 12 months of classification as held for sale (subject to limited exceptions)

5   The asset is being actively marketed for sale at a sales price reasonable in relation to its fair value

6   Actions required to complete the plan indicate that it is unlikely that plan will be significantly changed or withdrawn

We clearly intend to sell the equipment and if management puts in place plans to find a buyer including actively marketing the equipment at a reasonable price, then the equipment would be treated as "held for sale" and would be held at the lower of the carrying amount and the fair value less costs of disposal. Assets held for sale will be shown in the statement of financial position under current assets and will no longer be depreciated.

Equipment held in storage

The equipment which we have decided to store until a final decision should remain on the statement of financial position. According to IAS 16, relating to de-recognition, an asset should only be removed from the statement of financial position on disposal or when it is withdrawn from use and no future economic benefits are expected from the asset. In this case, the equipment which is held in storage may be used in the future to generate economic benefits. The equipment would also continue to be depreciated since according to IAS 16, depreciation begins when the asset is available for use and continues until the asset is derecognised, even if it is idle.

Exercise 3

Investment in RPA

Relevant costs

The depreciation costs and amortisation costs are not relevant costs as they are not cash flows. However, the purchase costs of the hardware and software and the development costs will be relevant costs.

The IT maintenance costs will be irrelevant as they relate to the cost of an existing employee who will be paid whether the investment in RPA goes ahead or not.

The licence fees will be a relevant cost as these are incremental costs.

The training costs are relevant costs as these are future, incremental cash flows. However, they are not likely to occur on an annual basis but on an ad-hoc basis as it is likely that further training will be required in the future for new employees and in the event of any changes to the software.

The savings on salaries and benefit for staff is relevant. It is not intended to make any of the existing staff redundant however by investing in RPA we avoid having to hire additional staff.

Other factors

The use of RPA will free accounting staff to concentrate on value-added processes which require analysis and evaluation including supporting business managers with decision making.

An automated process is available around the clock, and is able to scale up or down quickly, according to demand. The ability to manage demand due to business growth or cyclical volume peaks is easily achievable when RPA is implemented. This will enable us to meet peaks in demand by dedicating more resource to any process without recruitment, training requirements or overtime costs.

RPA eliminates human error and it also brings 24/7 operation with no downtime. Robots also never give their notice therefore there is savings in recruitment costs.

Beyond budgeting

Characteristics of beyond budgeting

Under a 'beyond budgeting' approach, rolling forecasts on a monthly or quarterly basis, are suggested as the main alternative to annual budgeting. Instead of evaluating performance against budget targets these are replaced with relative external performance measures which are based on a comparison of key performance indicators with competitors and similar units within the company.

Beyond budgeting supports decentralisation and employee empowerment. It also places greater emphasis on team-based rewards rather than individual rewards.

Benefits of adopting a beyond budgeting approach

One of the main problems with our current annual budgeting system is that it is rapidly out of date. We are operating under fast changing market conditions with competitors open new gyms on a regular basis and changes to technology impacting on customer preferences. The use of rolling forecasts would provide more accurate information that reflects the latest estimates on economic trends and customer demand. This would enable our managers to determine strategies that adapt to the fast changing market conditions.

The use of relative performance measures will shift the focus from beating other managers for resource allocation to beating the competition by creating a climate based on competitive success. For example, we could use relative performance measures to compare the performance of the gym managers and/or staff across the company. The use of comparative measures will also ensure that our managers strive for continuous improvement rather than being content to meet budget targets.

Beyond budgeting will motivate our managers by giving clear responsibilities and challenges.

Authority will be devolved to our operational managers who are closer to the action and so can react quickly. The managers will be empowered to deliver key ratios rather than to keep to strict budget limits. Our managers will have wider discretion in making decisions and can obtain resources without being dependent on resource allocation as part of the budget process. This will enable our managers to react quickly to seize any opportunities that arise as a result of the changing environment.

By making rewards team-based it will eliminate dysfunctional behaviour. The success of our company does not rely on one individual but in everyone working together to achieve the same goals. The success of the operation of each of the gyms is not solely reliant on the gym manager but on all the staff. As part of the process we can establish customer-orientated teams and create information systems which provide fast and open information throughout the organisation.

KPIs for gym staff

The following are suggested KPIs which we could use to measure the performance of our gym staff:

Number of new members

As most of our costs are fixed it is important to grow our membership to obtain economies of scale. The gym managers and staff are able to influence growth in new members through price promotion and by ensuring that feedback from existing members is positive.

Average membership fee

It is important to grow the number of members but profitable growth is fundamental. Price promotions and discount should be used by the gym managers with care to ensure profitable growth and also to avoid a price war with other local competitor gyms.

Number of member complaints

This is a measure of customer satisfaction and could be linked to the number of members leaving and therefore income. Measuring the number of complaints will ensure managers take care to manage those areas of the business that can result in complaints such as a lack of available staff or delays in mending broken equipment. Furthermore, when presented with issues, managers and staff will be more careful to ensure that these are resolved to the customer's satisfaction wherever possible.

Exercise 4

<u>Variance analysis</u>

Fee income price variance

The adverse fee income price variance relates solely to the full fee members since the fee for student members was in line with budget. This is at least partly due the decision to offer discounted membership fees as this was not reflected in the original budget. It will also be partly due to the discounting of the full fee by gym managers of the gyms that have been affected by the competitor company opening nearby gyms.

Fee income mix variance

The fee income mix variance measures the effect on fee income of the sales mix being different than budget. The variance is adverse which reflects the split between full fee members and student members. There is a higher percentage of student members than budgeted and as student members have a lower average fee the variance is adverse. It would be helpful to discover why the mix is different to budget. It may be that the mix assumed in the budget was inappropriate and if so, the budget for future period should be revised or the variance separated into its planning and operational elements. A further breakdown of membership numbers in each of the gyms would be useful.

Fee income quantity variance

The fee income quantity variance measures the effect on fee income of the total quantity being higher or lower than budget based on volumes at the budgeted mix. The total number of members per gym are below budget which will be partly as a result of the late opening of the new gyms and partly due to the competition from the competitor who may have attracted some of our existing and potential members to its gyms. The discounted fees which have been offered to full fee members both through the sales promotion and by the gym managers has failed to have the desired impact on full fee member numbers. The number of student members however is above budget despite the fact that fees were not discounted. This suggests that our budget estimates of student numbers were potentially inaccurate and that there may also be scope to increase the fee for student members. The student fee offered by GymFit may be lower than that offered by the competitor firm and this needs to be clarified.

Gym manager and staff's concerns

The gym staff's concerns are valid since it is unfair that the company's reward system is based on factors that they cannot control. The gyms staff would not have been able to influence the late opening of the gyms. It could be argued however that the gym managers were able to influence the impact of the competitor opening nearby gyms since they have the authority to adjust fee levels.

However, we do not want to get into a price war with the competitor company and we need to take action to avoid this happening. We could stop the GymFit managers from using indiscriminate discounting and perhaps offer, for example, a price match guarantee to match the membership fee of any gyms within a 2 mile radius of our gyms. Other types of promotion should also be considered, for example, offering additional free classes.

In future reporting, it may be better to split the variances between their operational and planning elements. The operational variances would then reflect the position relating to factors that are within the control of the operational managers and would be a better basis for the reward system.

Cash flow management

Dealing with the cash flow deficit

There are a number of steps that we could take to plan for any cash deficit arising including:

(a) Approaching the bank to arrange additional short-term borrowings or to increase overdraft facilities.

(b) The statement of financial position as at 31st December 2018 shows investments of C$200,000. Assuming we have not already done so, we could sell these although we would need to consider any penalties that may be imposed as a result of early withdrawal / sale;

(c) We could review the finance methods for our capital expenditure on gym equipment and /or the fit-out of new gyms. It may be possible to arrange different forms of finance or change / renegotiate the payments dates on the finance. For example, we may choose to lease the equipment rather than buy the equipment outright;

(d) We could also consider the timing of our dividend payment to shareholders;

(e) We could consider postponing revenue expenditure such as advertising expenditure. We should be careful however as whilst advertising expenditure tends to be classified as discretionary expenditure a reduction or delay in the expenditure may result in reduced member numbers at a later date;

(f) It may be possible to bring forward the planned disposal of non-current assets. If the asset is not required, we could sell the asset sooner or perhaps arrange with the purchaser to pay a deposit.

Why regular cash flow forecasting is important for GymFit

Regular cash flow forecasting would ensure that the forecasts are more accurate, reflecting for example, the latest expectations of the new gyms. Adoption of a rolling budget approach would be particularly suited to cash flow forecasts which needs to be reviewed regularly.

It is important at GymFit not just to focus on profit but also to improve cash flow management. Our costs are mainly fixed therefore any changes to member numbers will have a major impact on profit but also on cash flow.

A rolling approach to cash flow forecasting will offer better visibility of cash flows and help to identify deficits, thereby ensuring appropriate financing arrangements are put in place to avoid a shortage of funds. Visibility of cash will also allow GymFit managers to adjust the timing of planned expenditure to avoid any cash flow shortages.

Where the cash flow forecasts are suggesting that there will be a surplus, GymFit managers can arrange to reinvest these funds to make further gains.

Feedback on the real exam and tips on answering the more technical aspects of P1 and F1

Chapter learning objectives

To understand how to answer exam tasks that focus on the more technical areas of F1 and P1.

1 Summary of exams to date

1.1 Examiner's feedback

After each exam sitting CIMA publish the exams, suggested answers, summary marking guides and an examiner's report that discusses all variants from that sitting.

While many students are producing high quality scripts in the time available, there are common themes that have arisen where students can improve. Here are some typical comments:

- **Time pressure is not the main problem**

  "There was little evidence that time pressure caused any problems and most candidates completed answers for all tasks, although in some of the variants answers on specific elements of tasks were superficial or too brief... Often this seemed to be due to a lack of technical knowledge..."

- **No need for lengthy introductions**

  "Some candidates are wasting time giving extraneous information. There were often lengthy introductions to issues given which then meant that there was less time to address the actual task in hand. There are no marks for introductions or setting the scene; candidates need to address the task being asked and no more."

- **Planning answers is important**

  "When sitting an Operational level case study examination, it is important to take time to plan your answer so that you are able to apply your knowledge to the specifics of the case. I would suggest that for certain tasks you plan your answers in the answer screen itself.

  For example, if you are asked for the potential benefits and problems of a course of action, I would suggest that you first note down headings for benefits and problems. Then under each heading list your benefits and problems; these will become your sub-headings. Then you can write a short paragraph under each sub-heading.

  This will allow you time to think about all of the points that you want to make and will help to give your answer a clear format. Ultimately, it should save you time".

- **Apply models to the scenario**

  "There was evidence in a number of the variants of the erroneous use of learned models. In a case study the most important thing to do is to answer the task asked within the context of the business. The random inclusion of models with no application to the company, earned no marks."

- **Justify comments made**

  "Candidates also need to be conscious of unsupported assertions. Making statements such as, "this improves decision making", "this graph is essential" or "planning is enhanced" is not enough to gain any marks. Candidates must explain "how" the model or technique achieves these assertions. Wild enthusiasm is not enough without sound and reasoned explanation. As in November many candidate answers would have been improved if they added "because of ...." at the end of a sentence to explain why something is as it is."

- **Technical marks for P1 and F1 are often the biggest discriminator**

  "As is consistent with other exam sessions, the skill which was demonstrated the best was business skills, closely followed by people skills. Candidates seemed to be most comfortable using their knowledge from E1 to demonstrate applied business and people skills. Applying knowledge from P1 and especially F1 to demonstrate technical skills appeared to be more challenging."

  "Application to the scenario was generally good for tasks that linked to the E1 and P1 syllabi but often still poor in relation to F1 and the more technical aspects of P1."

2 Answering more technical aspects of P1

2.1 Introduction

As stated above, one of the main differentiators between students who pass and students who fail is answering the more technical aspects of F1 and P1.

In the next two sections we consider some examples of such tasks from the February 2016 exam.

2.2 The February 2016 exam

The pre-seen information for the February 2016 exam concerned a company called First Class Bakery (FCB), a cake and dessert manufacturer in the country of Beeland.

Key details were as follows:

- All products were currently sold within Beeland.

- Originally set up by three brothers, the company was now 20% owned by the one remaining brother, Frank Mitchell, who was also the MD, and 80% owned by Universal Foods, a large quoted group.

- First Class Bakery made three types of cake – slab cakes, special occasion cakes and desserts. Each went through three production processes – ingredient prep, mixing and baking and finishing – although the degree of labour involved depended on the product line.

- First Class Bakery had a good reputation for quality and VFM, although the bulk of its cakes were sold to large retailers with customers' own brand labels attached.

- Sales and profits fell in 2015, which was expected to some degree due to a declining market. However, in the case of First Class Bakery this also resulted in a considerable worsening of its cash position from cash in hand of B$870,000 at the start of the year to an overdraft of B$385,000 at the end.

- The company was also under-investing in non-current assets and seeing an increase in cash tied up in working capital.

Taking all these factors together, it could be argued that First Class Bakery was in serious need of new ideas to turn its fortunes around.

2.3 Variant 1 – section 4 – decision making under uncertainty

Scenario

- The company decided to bring out a new organic cherry slabcake.

- Four different contracts were being considered for the supply of the cherries from a new supplier called TOCC.

- Students were given a pay-off table and a regret table for each contract under three different demand projections.

Task

Students were asked to produce the following:

(1) An interpretation of the information included in the pay-off table

(2) An explanation of the Maximax, Maximin and Minimax Regret decision making criteria, including commentary on the risk attitudes of managers who employ such methods and identification of which contract would be selected under each of these decision criteria.

(3) An explanation of expected values and the potential benefits and problems of their use in the decision regarding the purchase of organic cherries.

Suggested answer approach/structure

Set up headings as suggested by the question requirement.

1   Interpretation of the pay-off table

- Start with technical knowledge – explain what a pay-off table shows but keep this part brief. Comments could include:

  "The pay-off table shows a measure of the value or 'pay-off' of each possible outcome in terms of the decision facing the directors."

  "A pay-off table can be a useful way to represent and analyse a scenario where there is a range of possible outcomes and responses."

  "A pay-off table illustrates all possible gains/losses and as such is often used in decision-making under conditions of uncertainty."

- Then apply this to FCB using the actual figures and scenario given.

  This is the most important aspect:

  "In our case there are four possible purchase levels for cherries from TOCC and there are three possible levels of demand from the customers."

  "The pay-off table shows the level of contribution that would be earned by First Class Bakery as a result of entering each of the alternative contracts depending on the level of demand from customers. The level of contribution would vary according to the contract size chosen."

- Try to develop points further by considering wider issues, implications and so on.

  "The price of organic cherries reduces as the contract size increases and therefore the contribution per cake would increase."

  "In situations where the contract size is greater than the level of customer demand then surplus cakes will be sold to local farmers."

- Developing your answer could also include judgement/scepticism/limitations of the method – for example,

  "The value of the table is very much dependent on the accuracy of the market research that has been undertaken."

2 Explanation of Maximax, Maximin and Minimax Regret

- For each method plan an approach, starting with technical knowledge and then applying to FCB.

  One such plan could be as follows:

  (1) Explain basic approach

  (2) Explain the underlying assumption

  (3) Link to risk attitudes

  (4) What decision should FCB make?

- Applying this to Maximax, for example, gives the following:

  Technical knowledge:

  Basic approach – "The Maximax rule to decision making involves selecting the decision option that would maximise the maximum pay-off potentially achievable."

  Underlying assumption – "It is based on the assumption that the best pay-off will occur."

  Link to risk attitudes – "This approach to decision making would be appropriate for a decision maker who has an optimistic approach to decision making and is prepared to select the decision option that would yield the best results if the most beneficial decision outcome were to occur."

  Application to FCB – decision backed up with data specific to the scenario:

  "Under the Maximax decision criterion Contract D would be selected since it might result in the highest possible contribution of B$744,000"

  This can then be repeated for the other two methods.

3   Explanation of expected values.

* The use of EVs:

   "The expected value is calculated by weighting each of the contribution levels by its associated probability.

   The sum of these weighted amounts is called the expected value of the probability distribution.

   In other words the expected value is the weighted arithmetic mean of the possible outcomes"

* Potential benefits:

   "Expected values are associated with risk neutrality and consider the probability of each possible outcome.

   The decision information is reduced to and represented by a single number that facilitates decision making.

   The calculations are relatively straightforward."

* Potential problems:

   "The probabilities used are usually very subjective because two individuals will not necessarily assign the same probabilities to a particular outcome.

   The expected value is merely a weighted average and therefore has little relevance for a one-off decision.

   The expected value does not necessarily correspond to any of the actual possible outcomes as in this decision".

Examiner's comments

Most of task 4 was reasonably well answered.

Interpreting the information in the payoff table was not well answered though. Many answers were brief and indeed a significant number of candidates missed it altogether. It would appear that candidates think that this is more complicated than it actually is.

A candidate who commented that there were four contracts being considered (each with a different purchase price for the cherries), that there were three possible levels of demand (hence uncertainty) and that each of the cells represented the contribution from each contract under each of the possible levels of demand, would have scored at least half marks. Those that commented about the fact that the contract choice was the decision and that the possible demand levels were outside of managements control, as well as commenting about the impact of the cherry price on contribution would have scored more marks again.

The explanation of the decision using maximax, maximin and minimax regret was well answered: candidates seem well prepared for this and many scored full marks. Most candidates were able to comment on expected value well but often the benefits and problems were only superficially addressed.

2.4   Variant 3 – section 4 – break even analysis including a graph

Scenario

- The company decided to bring out a new range of Gluten Absent (GA) products.

- Directors concerned about risk – especially whether the new products will break even.

- Students were given a multi-product break even chart with supporting tables of information.

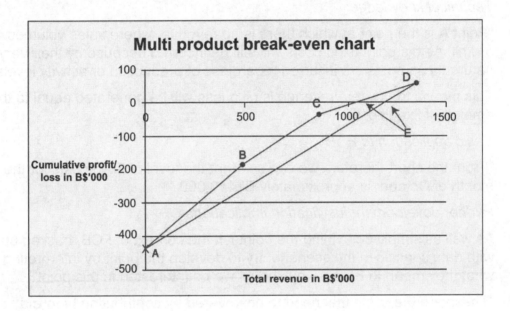

Task

Students were then asked to explain the following:

(1)   What various points on the graph represented and what the two main lines were

(2)   The usefulness of the chart to FCB.

Note: there was a third aspect to the task that looked at working capital management but we will focus on the P1 aspects here.

Suggested answer approach/structure

Set up headings as suggested by the question requirement.

1   Interpretation of the chart

- Based on your technical knowledge you should be able to understand what each point represented. As well as explaining this, you would need to apply your comments to FCB by incorporating actual figures and details from the chart given in the scenario.

- For example, point A was where there were zero sales. Comments could include:

Technical knowledge:

"Point A is the point at which there is no revenue, where sales volumes are nil. At this point fixed costs will still be incurred because by their very nature these costs are incurred regardless of production or activity levels.

This means that where revenue is nil a loss will be generated equal to the amount of fixed costs. "

Basic application to FCB

"From the chart therefore we can see that the level of fixed costs for the month of October is approximately B$440,000."

Further development/justification/implications

As well as simply describing the points in the context of FCB, backed up with data specific to the scenario, try to develop the point by interpreting what they mean to FCB – why should we be interested in this point?

"These are the costs that need to be covered by contribution before a profit can be made."

- Similarly, point(s) E represented break-even:

Technical knowledge:

"Point E is the break-even point on each line."

Basic application:

"Looking at the chart one can see that the break-even point (the point at which neither a profit nor a loss is expected to be made) on the straight line is where revenue is approximately B$1,225,000.

Further development

Here we can do more to interpret what the figures mean to FCB

"This means that revenue can fall to this level from the expected level of B$1,356,000 before we reach the point where fixed costs are not covered by contribution."

- Next you had to comment on why there were two lines

  This was harder as you needed to recognise that one line assumed selling products in constant mix but the other allowed us to sell in the order of highest C/S ratio.

  "The line between points A and D represents the expected profit or loss at different revenue levels assuming that the mix of sales that we expect is kept the same regardless of the level of total revenue."

  "In other words each point on the line represents sales revenue being comprised of 37% from sales of lemon cakes, 34% from sales of carrot cakes and 29% from sales of coffee cakes."

  "The line which connects points A, B, C and D is the line that represents the relationship between revenue and profit or loss on the assumption that we sell the cakes in order of profitability (measured as the c/s ratio)."

- Note that the answer here is applied to the scenario. Indeed it could have been expanded further to give the order in which the cakes were assumed to be sold (carrot, coffee and then lemon).

2   The usefulness of this multi-product break-even chart

- Make sure you consider both sides of the argument and try to justify/develop points.

- For example, when arguing that the chart is useful, you could develop your argument as follows:

  Technical knowledge:

  "The chart is useful because it gives an idea of the level of revenue at which we will make neither a profit nor a loss."

  Application:

  "This is particularly relevant in our case because these are new products in what is a new and specialised market for us and therefore we do not have experience at forecasting sales volumes."

  Development:

  "The sales team have given their best estimates for the month of October, but there is no past experience to base this on, which means that its accuracy is questionable."

Examiner's comments

In the first element of task 4 most candidates made a sensible attempt at explaining each of the points A, B, C, D and E and most were able to identify A as the fixed costs (although many did not state what those fixed costs were from the chart). There was some confusion on the other points however (especially points B and C), although some candidates did achieve full marks here. Many candidates were not able to comment on the differences between the two lines. Answers in respect of the usefulness of break-even in this situation were mixed. Most did not comment that a margin of safety could be established and the majority of answers were very generic.

2.5 Variant 4 – section 1 – linear programming, including a graph

Scenario

- The company was negotiating a large order with a major customer.

- If successful, then production capacity would be expanded in the long term. However, in the short term (the next 3 months) the company had to deal with a number of constraints. These were described but not given in mathematical terms.

- Students were given a linear programming graph (with various lines labelled), along with various equations and supporting tables of information.

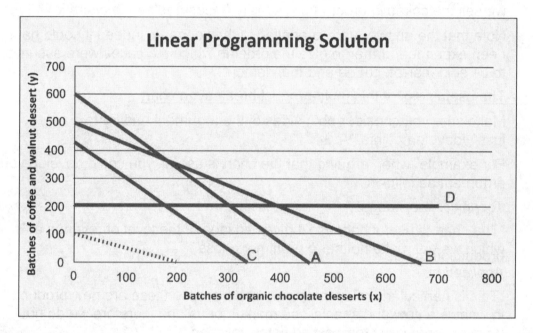

Task

Students were then asked to prepare a briefing note that:

(1) Interpreted the linear programming graph

(2) Explained the usefulness of the graph to FCB.

Suggested answer approach/structure

This would have been very tricky had you forgotten basic technical knowledge concerning linear programming! As stated earlier, no topics are off-limits to the examiner.

1   Interpretating the graph

- Planning your approach is more critical here than in some other requirements as there are many components to linear programming that need to be incorporated.

  With the break-even chart covered in the previous section the requirement specifically asked for comments on each labelled point on the chart. Here it doesn't explicitly ask that but it would wise to incorporate such explanations in your answer and identify what each line represents.

  Linear programming has a well defined series of steps, so a very good approach (and structure) would be to walk through the method:

  (1)   identify/explain constraints,

  (2)   identify/explain the feasible region,

  (3)   identify/explain the objective function/iso-contribution line,

  (4)   identify the optimal solution and interpret.

- Based on your technical knowledge you should be able to link the narrative concerning constraints with the equations given and hence identify which line represents which constraint.

  "Each line on the graph represents a potential constrained resource to our production of the new dessert flavours: line A relates to unrefined sugar, line B to labour hours, line C to machine hours and line D to demand for the coffee and walnut flavour."

  "Each of the lines A, B and C represents the different combinations of production of x (batches of organic chocolate) and y (batches of coffee and walnut) that will utilise all of the resource and hence represents the maximum production under each resource."

  "Line D is a demand constraint line."

- With the different steps in linear programming, you can give a general comment based on technical knowledge and then apply to the scenario. For example, considering the idea of the feasible region:

  Technical knowledge:

  "In order to interpret the graph we need to identify the 'feasible region' of production. The feasible region is the area on the graph contained within all of the constraint lines (which are lines A, B, C and D). In situations where there are several constraints (as in this case), the feasible region will be the area below each of the lines that is common to all constraints."

  "The reason the feasible region is below the lines and not above the lines is because these lines represent the maximum production or demand of x and y given the constraint in place, hence it is only possible to have production below the line and not above it."

Basic application

"In our graph, the feasible region (which remember is the area below each line which is common to all) is the area below both line C and line D, which means that line C (the machine hours constraint) and line D (the sales volume for coffee and walnut desserts constraint) are our binding constraints."

Further development/explanation

"The optimum solution for the production of organic chocolate and coffee and walnut desserts must therefore be in this feasible area, because it is only at production within this area that we will have enough machine hours and demand for the coffee and walnut desserts."

2 The usefulness of the linear programming graph

- Make sure you consider both sides of the argument and try to justify/develop points.

- For example, when arguing that the approach is useful, you could develop your argument as follows:

Technical knowledge:

"The linear programming graph is a useful tool in situations like this where there are a number of potential resource constraints on production, as it does identify the optimum solution where contribution will be maximised within the boundaries of the constraints."

Application:

"In our case: production of 200 batches of coffee and walnut and 180 batches of organic chocolate."

Development

Given this is an argument, make sure you consider counter arguments/limitations and so on:

"However, whilst this is the production plan that in theory maximises contribution, this ignores other factors such as customer requirements."

"Also, a linear programming solution is only ever sensible for a very short term production decision or within a small range of production. This is because over time and volumes the nature of costs can change, Linear programming works on the assumption of linearity, and therefore ignores changes over time and economies of scale."

Examiner's comments

> Task 1 was the most poorly answered part of this variant.
>
> Few candidates appeared to be familiar with linear programming; Indeed many confused it with either linear regression or breakeven analysis. This is quite worrying as this subject should have been learned while studying P1.
>
> For those candidates that did interpret the linear programming graph, the majority noted that lines A, B, C, D represented the constraints.
>
> However, only a few candidates noted that the binding constraints were represented by lines C and D. There was little attempt to explain the feasible region, the iso-contribution line or to conclude about the optimal solution. Few candidates produced anything but the most superficial analysis and therefore scored very poorly.
>
> In the second element of the task two things are worthy of note. Firstly, if asked to explain how useful a model is to a business, the analysis should include a balanced argument, otherwise how can its usefulness be assessed? Most candidates only considered the benefits of linear programming. Secondly, stating "it is very useful "is not enough, even if this is qualified by "as it will improve management decision making". To get a good mark a candidate needs to explain how management decision making is improved.

3 Answering more technical aspects of F1

3.1 Introduction

As stated above, one of the main differentiators between students who pass and students who fail is answering the more technical aspects of F1 and P1.

In the last section we considered some P1 tasks from the February 2016 exam. Here we look at some F1 tasks from February 2017 that caused particular difficulties for candidates.

3.2 The February 2017 exam

The pre-seen information for the February 2017 exam concerned a company called Mavis Venderby ("Mavis"), which made and sold flat-pack wooden bee hives in the European country of Tucland,

Key details were as follows:

- All products were currently sold within Tucland.

- Mavis sold through three channels – a store next to the factory (20%), a website (45%) and via telephone sales (35%).

- Mavis had a strong brand with a reputation for high quality beehives.

- Mavis made four types of hive and foundation but outsourced the manufacture of frames. It did not sell polystyrene hives, beekeeping equipment, live bees or offer beekeeping courses. All of these could be considered to be potential areas for expansion.

- Revenue had fallen by 0.3% in 2016, which combined with an increase in cost of sales, resulted in a fall in operating profit of over 20% on a like for like basis. The company had recently acquired new premises, so the time was ripe for new product development.

- The company's year-end is 28 February.

3.3 Variant 1 – section 4 – IAS 10 and IAS 2

Scenario

- Mavis had introduced a new hive made from polystyrene that had proved to be extremely successful.

- It is now September 2017 and a major customer that had bought 200 hives in January 2017 had gone into liquidation. This seemed to come as a surprise despite the customer having not paid, either by the year-end or by the date of the email.

- One of the directors suggested changing the method of inventory valuation from standard costing to LIFO, FIFO or weighted average instead. He believed that, as there was inflation in the economy, this would save corporation tax.

Task

Students were asked to produce a briefing paper on the following:

(1) A P1 task on C/S ratios – not discussed here

(2) How the liquidation would affect Mavis' financial statements, plus any implications for receivables management.

(3) Whether the change in inventory valuation method was allowed and the potential impact on the financial statements

Suggested answer approach/structure

Set up headings as suggested by the question requirement.

<u>Impact of liquidation on financial statements</u>

- A common problem with more detailed financial reporting tasks is that students fail to incorporate all the factors they should but focus on just the main one or two. Given this, it is worth planning the key issues that should come out of your technical knowledge.

  Issues here include the following:

  (1) The obvious issue is that the debt may/will have to be written off

  (2) The more subtle issue that many students miss is whether this also qualifies as an adjusting event under IAS 10: Events after the reporting date (it does!).

(3) In terms of receivables management there are two possible angles you could take – firstly what additional financial reporting issues there may be, such as the need to review all other receivables balances to estimate the year end figure. Secondly, what other changes are needed to receivables management, such as the production of aged receivables reports.

This could form the basis of an answer structure.

- *Technical knowledge.*

  Comments could include:

  "IAS 10: Events after the reporting date, states that where there is evidence that a condition existed at the reporting period date and the financial statements have not yet been approved by the director, those financial statements should be adjusted to reflect the change."

- *Application.*

  "Although the customer was not declared insolvent until many months after the reporting period date of 28 February 2017, the debt owed relates to sales made in the year leading up to that date. Within our draft financial statements for the year ended 28 February 2017 there is a receivable balance for this customer (the conditions) and we now have evidence that this money is not going to be collected. In accordance with IAS 10 this is an adjusting event."

- *Further development*

  Make sure you answer the question and address the impact on the financial statements:

  "In terms of the impact on our financial statements we will need to reduce the receivables balance by the amount that the customer owes and debit the irrecoverable debt expense in the statement of profit or loss (which will increase administrative expenses)."

- *Inventory management – FR aspects*

  "The implication of this for our receivables management is that we need to ensure that we review all receivables balances (both at 28 February 2017 and now) for any other amounts that might not be recovered."

- *Inventory management – practical aspects*

  "This debt has been outstanding for many months and it would appear that it was a surprise that had not been paid. Possibly as a result of all the changes to the business and the increased workload regarding credit customers, monitoring of receivables balances has been ignored. We need to ensure that an aged receivables report is prepared, reviewed and acted on regularly."

Change in inventory valuation

- As before, the danger with this task is that students limit the scope of their answers.

  (1) The obvious issue is that IAS 2: Inventories allows the weighted average and FIFO methods to value inventory but not LIFO.

  (2) The more subtle issue is that the director is suggesting a change in an accounting policy, so you need to widen the discussion to include IAS 8: Accounting Policies, Changes in Accounting Estimates and Errors.

  (3) You could also consider whether it is ethical to change an accounting policy to pay less tax

Again you need to think of an answer structure. For example:

- Is the change allowed?

  Technical knowledge:

  "IAS 2: Inventories allows the weighted average and FIFO methods to value inventory but not LIFO.

  IAS 8: Accounting Policies, Changes in Accounting Estimates and Errors, states that a change of this nature is a change in accounting policy, which if allowed would require a retrospective adjustment to the financial statements. subsidiary, then acquisition accounting will apply."

  Basic application to Mavis:

  "Changes in accounting policy are only permitted if required by a standard or if it results in the financial statements providing more reliable and more relevant information. We will need to assess if this is the case.

  Further development/implications:

  "Currently we use standard costs to value inventory in our financial statements and in accordance with IAS 2 these will need to be adjusted by a share of the variances at the year end to give an approximation of cost. If either FIFO or weighted average give us a better approximation for cost then it is possible that the auditors will agree this change."

- Impact on financial statements

  Technical knowledge:

  "IAS 8 means that, as well as restating the year-end valuations, we would have to restate the inventory value using the weighted average or FIFO method for the comparatives in the financial statements as well as the opening position in retained earnings."

  Basic application to Mavis

  "The impact of changing to the FIFO method of valuation on the financial statements would be to increase the recorded value of the inventory at the year end. The weighted average method of valuation is likely to give a similar recorded value to the standard cost.

The impact on profit will also depend upon the opening inventory position (as this will also change).

Further development/implications:

"In any event any profit differences are only temporary as the closing inventory for this February 2017 will be the opening inventory for the year ended 28 February 2018. In the long term there is no tax benefit."

- Ethical issue

  One final point is that it is not ethical to manipulate profits in order to pay less taxation. Even if there was a tax benefit (which in the long term there isn't) this could be seen as tax avoidance, which although not illegal, is viewed negatively.

Examiner's comments

In the second element of this task some candidates grasped the issue, had knowledge of the relevant accounting standard, and earned good marks. However most candidates demonstrated a lack of financial accounting knowledge, and typically ignored the requirement to discuss the financial accounting impact. They instead wrote all they knew about factoring, cash flow management and aged receivables analysis which earned relatively few marks.

The final element of this task was by far the worst attempted part of this case study. Many candidates failed to recognise that LIFO could not be used for financial reporting, and not many considered the ethics of trying to manipulate the tax bill in this way. By far the most common mistake however, was to explain (and even this was often inaccurate) the basic principles of FIFO, LIFO and AVCO without applying this to the question asked.

3.4 Variant 2 – section 1 – Impairment (IAS 36) and IAS 2

Scenario

- On the night of 28 February a major storm damaged a fork lift truck and all of the cedar hives in inventory.

- The truck is still functional despite being dented and scratched, half of the hives are a complete write-off and the other half could be made serviceable and sold, albeit at about half the normal price.

Task

Students were then asked to explain how the damage to the finished goods inventory and fork-lift truck would be affect the financial statements for the year ended 28 February 2017.

Note: there was another aspect to the task that looked at using linear programming to devise an optimal production plan but we will focus on the F1 aspect here.

Suggested answer approach/structure

- Unlike the previous example, the main problem here was that many students over-complicated the question and tried to include far too much in the time available (especially standards that were irrelevant), resulting in incomplete, sketchy answers. Planning is thus essential.

  Often with such tasks you will need to set up the answer structure based on the rules within the relevant accounting standard, so it is vital that you still know the level of detail required.

- Based on your F1 technical knowledge, you should recognise that we are looking at two distinct issues:

  (1) Inventory – IAS2: Inventory states that inventory should be valued at the lower of cost and net realisable value (NRV).

  (2) Fork-lift truck – IAS 36 Impairment of Assets seeks to ensure that an entity's assets are not carried at more than their recoverable amount (i.e. the higher of fair value less costs of disposal and value in use).

- This could form the basis of your plan and, therefore, answer structure.

1   Inventory

- When applying accounting standards it is always worth starting with a basic statement of the relevant rule or principle.

  "The fundamental principle of IAS2: Inventory, is that inventory should be stated at the lower of cost and net realisable value (NRV)."

- Then apply the concept/rules

  "The storm has caused a physical deterioration in the cedar finished goods inventory and therefore it is likely that NRV is less than cost. Indeed, at least half of our cedar box and slatted hives are now worthless and therefore these should now be excluded from the valuation of the stock counted inventory.

  The effect of this is that our finished goods inventory value will be lower than would otherwise have been the case.

  This has the effect of increasing cost of sales for the year ended 28 February 2017 as closing inventory will be lower than it should be. In effect the inventory will be written off, which will reduce profit for the year, as this is wasted production."

- Make sure you answer the question and include the serviceable hives

  "For the rest of the inventory which can be salvaged we need to consider its NRV. Given that we are likely to be able to sell for half of our normal price, NRV will be lower than cost. NRV is the estimated sales price less estimated costs of completion less estimated costs necessary to make the sale.

  The estimated selling price is going to be much lower than our usual price: a good estimate would be the price any of our competitors charge for non-perfect products (assuming they do). Alternatively Jacinta, Joseph or Toby may already have a price in mind; ultimately it will depend just how damaged the hives are.

The estimated costs of completion will be the costs of making the hives serviceable. This will include any materials required and labour costs. The estimated costs necessary to make the sale will be the cost of the usual packaging, distribution costs and any other costs that might need to be incurred in order to sell the damaged hives.

The effect in our financial statements for the year ended 28 February 2017 is the same as for the inventory that is worthless, although the effect will be smaller because we will be able to record the inventory at NRV."

2 <u>Fork-lift truck</u>

- *Technical knowledge – statement of rule*

"IAS 36 Impairment of Assets seeks to ensure that an entity's assets are not carried at more than their recoverable amount (i.e. the higher of fair value less costs of disposal and value in use)."

- *Application with justification*

"An impairment loss will arise if the carrying amount of the fork lift truck exceeds its recoverable amount.

Carrying amount is the amount at which the fork-lift truck is included within property, plant and equipment, which will be its cost less accumulated depreciation to 28 February 2017.

Recoverable amount is the higher of the fork-lift truck's fair value less cost to sell and its value in use.

The fair value in the case of our fork lift truck would be the amount that we could sell it for in its current condition while the value in use is the present value of the future cash flows, expected to be derived from using the fork lift truck in the business.

As the fork lift truck is likely to generate the same future cash inflows as it did before the storm damage; hence its value in use is unchanged; it is likely that there is no requirement to impair the asset.

Therefore the damage will have no effect on the financial statements for the year ended 28 February 2017.

- *Other issues / wider discussion*

Any repair costs will be treated as expenses when incurred."

Examiner's comments

The first element of this task concerned the effect of damaged inventory and a damaged non-current asset on the financial statements.

This was intended to be a gentle and straightforward introduction to the variant, one that required the ability to apply IAS 2 and IAS 36.

Many candidates over-complicated the situation citing: IAS 2, IAS 7, IAS 8, IAS 10, IAS 16, IAS 18 and IAS 36. Rather than the structured and focused answered expected, the markers read long rambling and largely irrelevant answers that could only earn minimal marks.

3.5 Variant 3 – section 4 – IAS 16

Scenario

- The company has increased its range of products and won new customers, resulting in a new production facility and staff recruitment.

- One aspect of the expansion in capacity was building work in an old grain barn.

- A schedule of costs was given in the reference materials.

Task

Students were asked to explain what expenditure relating to the new production facility could be capitalised and what could not

Suggested answer approach/structure

- Based on your F1 technical knowledge, you should recognise that we are looking at IAS 16: Property, Plant and Equipment. This states that expenditure can be capitalised if it is either part of the purchase price or directly attributable to getting the asset ready for its intended use.

- For each cost in the schedule you would need to discuss whether or not the rule above has been met and why. It is not enough to say a rule has been met without any explanation or justification.

- *Technical knowledge – statement of rule*

  "IAS 16: Property, Plant and Equipment states that expenditure associated with an item of property plant and equipment can be capitalised if it is either part of the purchase price (including import duties) or directly attributable to getting the asset ready for its intended use."

  Application with justification

  "From the schedule the purchase price of the new plant and equipment, import duties and building contractor's cost all into this first category.

  The costs that are directly attributable costs include: the architects fees, the site preparation costs, and the installation of the plant and equipment. All of these costs are necessary to build and to ensure that the machines work correctly.

  The training costs however cannot be capitalised as they do not meet the definition of an asset. Although the training may lead to future economic benefit for our business, we cannot control it as the staff are free to leave the business at any time.

  The cost of marketing and general overhead are not likely to be directly attributable and will have to be expensed as they are incurred. The marketing is an event that bears no relation to the construction of the new facility and the overhead is an apportionment rather than directly incurred, which in accordance with IAS 16 cannot be capitalised."

Examiner's comments

Unfortunately, the final element of the task was very poorly answered.

Few candidates were able to explain what constituted the cost of property, plant and equipment as defined in IAS16 and therefore which of the costs given in the schedule could be capitalised.

Many candidates listed the costs given in the schedule and stated whether they could be capitalised without giving any explanation.

Some candidates, who were able to correctly explain which costs should be capitalised, then struggled to explain why the others should not be capitalised: saying that training, marketing and general overheads were revenue items was not sufficient to gain marks.

4 Final tips

Finally, the examiner has given the following advice for candidates:

- **Application**

  Application to the scenario is key to achieving a good mark.

  Simply reproducing rote-learned answers or pure knowledge of a topic area will score very few, if any, marks.

  Similarly taking a scatter gun approach to an issue and commenting on everything that you know about it from a theoretical point of view will score few marks.

- **Planning**

  When sitting an Operational level case study examination, it is important to take time to plan your answer so that you are able to apply your knowledge to the specifics of the case. I would suggest that for certain tasks you plan your answers in the answer screen itself.

  For example, if you are asked for the potential benefits and problems of outsourcing a particular function, I would suggest that you first note down headings for benefits and problems.

  Then under each heading list your benefits and problems; these will become your sub-headings.

  Then you can write a short paragraph under each sub-heading. This will allow you time to think about all of the points that you want to make and will help to give your answer a clear format.

  Ultimately, it should save you time.

- **The pre-seen material**

  Preparation on the pre-seen material is vital.

  Ensure that you are very familiar with the business, especially the financial information, before the exam as this will help you with applying your knowledge and will save you time.

  Similarly, an awareness of the industry that the business is in will help you to think of the wider issues that might impact on decisions that you could be asked to comment on.

- **Know the syllabus content relating to each of the core activities within the blueprint**

  Each variant of the Operational level case study examination will cover all core activities.

  Make sure that you do not leave topic areas out of your preparation.

  Given previous comments in this report and other reports, it is evident that F1 knowledge of financial reporting standards is poor. Please pay special attention to this.

- **Justify your comments**

  Be prepared to give balanced arguments or appraisals.

  Quite often you will be asked whether a tool or technique is appropriate to the business – it is just as likely to be suitable as not suitable.